Micro- and Small Enterprises as Vehicles for Poverty Reduction, Employment Creation and Business Development: The Ethiopian Experience

Tegegne Gebre-Egziabher
and
Meheret Ayenew

FSS Research Report No. 6.

fSS

Forum for Social Studies (FSS)
Addis Ababa

Printed in Addis Ababa

ISBN 978-99944-50-38-1

Forum for Social Studies (FSS)
P.O. Box 25864 code 1000
Addis Ababa, Ethiopia
Email: fss@ethionet.et
Web: www.fssethiopia.org.et

This Report was published with the financial support of the Department for International Development (DfID, UK), the Embassy of Ireland, the Royal Embassy of Denmark, and the Royal Embassy of Norway.

Contents

List of Abbreviations

ADB	African Development Bank
ASCI	Amhara Saving and Credit Institution
BBS	Basic business skills
BDS	Business Development Services
CEFE	Creation of enterprises through the formation of entrepreneurs
CPOs	Certified Payment Orders
DCSI	Department of Cottage and Small Industry
EB	Ethiopian Birr
EPRDF	Ethiopian Peoples Revolutionary Democratic Front
FeM&SEDA	Federal Micro- and Small Enterprises Development Agency
GDP	Gross Domestic Product
HASEDA	Handicrafts and Small-Scale Enterprises Development Agency
IEDI	Industrial Enterprise Development Institute
IHDP	Integrated Housing Development Program
ILO	International Labor Organization
IYB	Improve your business
MCIA	Ministry of Commerce, Industry and Crafts
MEDEP	Micro-enterprise Development Program
MoTI	Ministry of Trade and Industry
MoWUD	Ministry of Works and Urban Development
MSE	Micro- and Small Enterprise
NGOs	Non-governmental organizations
PASDEP	Plan for Accelerated and Sustainable Development to End Poverty
PLCs	Private limited companies

SNNPR	Southern Nations, Nationalities, and Peoples Region
SPSS	Statistical Package for the Social Sciences
SYB	Start your business
TET	Training of entrepreneurs training
WED	Women entrepreneurs development
UNCTAD	United Nations Conference on Trade and Development
USAID	United States Agency for International Development
VAT	Value Added Tax

List of Figures and Tables

1. Introduction

1.1. Background and Statement of the Problem

In many countries, there is now a wide recognition of the contribution of micro- and small enterprises (MSEs) to economic growth. In a cross-section of both developed and emerging economies, the contribution of the MSE sector to total employment, entrepreneurship and innovation cannot be underestimated. For example, this sector generates about 6.2 percent of the aggregate employment in the United States, 22.3 percent in China, about 80 percent in India, 67 percent in Japan and about 70 percent in EU countries (Carter and Jones-Evans 2004). To further underscore the social and economic importance of micro- and small enterprises, one UN study indicated that the sector represented 99 percent of all enterprises and provided around 65 million jobs in EU countries (UNCTAD 2005).

The potential advantages of a dynamic MSE sector have generated high expectations in many developing countries about the contributions of this sector to job creation and poverty reduction. Add to this the optimism that the full development of the MSE sector can foster competitiveness in the economy and achieve a more equitable distribution of the benefits of economic growth in both developed and developing economies. Such considerations have motivated many governments to put in place national policies to stimulate the growth of this sector in service, distribution and manufacturing-related economic activities.

Throughout the 1950s and 1960s, the currently vibrant Asian economies greatly benefited from the growth of the MSE sector. Governments of these nations pursued a strategic focus on export-oriented, medium-sized enterprises that fuelled the overall industrialization process and helped penetrate the international market place. The secrets of success lay in the fact that these firms were adept at applying technology and training to address the needs of growing markets. Additional success factors include mutually cooperative inter-firm relationships that led to exchanges of information and know-how and thus rendered individual firms less prone to risks, not to mention government support in technological extension services, including research support and information on sources of technology and encouraging linkages and networking among enterprises (UNCTAD 2005; Kula, Choudhary and Batzdorff 2005).

Given the enormous differences between the socio-economic background of the Asian countries and other developing nations, a direct replica of Asian experiences may not be a realistic option. With this proviso, however, it is extremely important that developing countries take useful cues from the Asian experience in their attempt to develop the MSE sector and make it a robust engine of economic growth and employment creation. In this regard, recommended steps include appropriate macroeconomic policies; an outward orientation with a focus on export promotion; measures to attract foreign direct investment; and effective selective interventions. In addition, adequate institutional capacity to formulate and implement appropriate economic policies, undertaking selective interventions and attracting foreign direct investment; and an efficient infrastructure to ensure sustained economic growth are also suggested as essential options (Hawkins 1998).

From the perspective of developing countries, MSEs have a number of advantages that make them attractive in accelerating economic growth. First, because MSEs are fairly labor intensive, employment opportunities are generated with a relatively low capital cost, a factor with limited supply in many developing nations. Secondly, they utilize raw materials and labor-intensive technology that are domestically available. Thirdly, policies and programs can be put in place to encourage the development of these industries in different parts of the country thereby reducing concentration of enterprises in certain areas and promoting balanced economic growth. Fourthly, manageable production capacity and their flexibility make them suitable to respond to current national demand and the limited size of the market in many developing nations (Fasika and Daniel 1997; Andualem 2004).

MSEs can contribute tremendously to the growth of national economies. However, many developing countries have not been lucky to benefit from the growth of this sector mainly due to institutional and policy constraints. Ill-conceived development strategies; a complex legal and regulatory environment that stifles the growth of the sector; shortage of adequate business development services, including lack of access to finance, markets and business skills and appropriate technology are to be blamed for lack of success.

Within the Ethiopian context, despite the potential contribution of the MSEs to poverty reduction and employment creation, the Government had not, until very recently, extended adequate support to the development of the sector. Simply put, there has not been meaningful government support in terms of recognition and access to finance and skills required for operating small businesses and enterprises profitably and efficiently (UNCTAD 2005; Eshetu and Zeleke 2008). This has meant that this sector is at its infancy and therefore needs a major institutional and resource boost to contribute to the country's program of sustainable development and poverty reduction.

On the other hand according to the Household Income, Consumption and Expenditure Survey (HICES) of 2004/05, urban poverty incidence has increased from about 33% in 1995/96 to about 35.1% in 2004/05. At present, the urban unemployment rate stands at a staggering 25 per cent of the employable population.

These two hard realities have forced the government of Ethiopia to turn to the MSE sector as a strategy that can have a lasting effect on reducing urban poverty, creating employment and bringing about overall growth in the business sector. As per the Government's PASDEP, the plan is to reduce urban unemployment through support for small and micro-enterprises and acceleration of the creation of urban-based employment, including vocational and technical training programs, a community-based and labor-intensive urban works program; expanding micro-finance institutions; and providing market support and service premises for small and micro-enterprises.

This is also reflected in the national urban development policy which has two main packages:

i) the urban development package; and
ii) the urban good governance package

The objectives of the urban development package are to reduce unemployment and poverty, to improve the capacity of the construction industry, to alleviate the existing housing problems, to promote urban areas as engines of economic growth and to improve urban social and economic infrastructure particularly for youth. Among the package's five pillars, micro-/small enterprise development program is the major one.

The micro- and small enterprise development program under the urban development package (2006) has the following objectives.

- To reduce urban poverty and unemployment by supporting micro- and small scale enterprises;

- To achieve fast growth through the creation of linkages between micro- and small enterprises with medium and large enterprises;

- To facilitate the growth and expansion of micro- and small enterprises and create a foundation for industrial development; and

- To promote the economic linkages between rural and urban areas.

The development of micro- and small businesses therefore has been touted as a vehicle to reduce poverty and create jobs for the increasing number of graduates out of the nation's technical and vocational education training institutes. Accordingly, the Government has earmarked significant resources for the expansion of the MSE sector in the different Regions.

This program has set ambitious goals to attack urban poverty and reduce unemployment in the urban areas of the country. Among other things, it planned to create employment opportunities for 1.5 million residents in 825 towns over the period 2006/07-09/10. According to the program, 50% of these beneficiaries will be women; and the Government plans to invest Birr 6.2 billion and provide 4900 hectares of land for MSE development.

While the government's intention and policy are in the right direction, it is necessary to examine the effects of the policy and the extent to which the policy has achieved its objectives of employment creation, poverty reduction and business growth in a sustainable way. Evidence in this regard is hard to come by. To date, there has not been an independent assessment of the contribution of the MSE development strategy to poverty reduction, job creation and business growth either at the federal or Regional levels. To fill the gap, the Forum for Social Studies (FSS) commissioned this study in 2009 to assess the benefits and long-term sustainability of the strategy as well as the businesses/enterprises that have been set up by the large number of entrepreneurs. The aim is to provide policy inputs that can help create a vibrant and dynamic MSE sector and enhance its potential contribution to the country's overall development.

1.2. Research Objectives

The general objective of the research is to assess the contribution of the micro- and small-scale enterprises strategy to poverty reduction, job creation and business development in selected major cities.

The specific objectives of the research are the following:

i) To examine the micro- and small enterprise strategy and its implementation;

ii) To identify the employment and poverty reduction impact of the MSEs strategy;

iii) To assess the extent to which the MSEs are showing dynamic trends in their growth and development; and

iv) To identify the challenges and constraints the MSE program and MSEs face in their operation.

1.3. Research Questions

i) What are the elements of the micro- and small enterprises strategy and the modalities of their implementation?

ii) What are the magnitudes and kinds of jobs being created by micro- and small enterprises?

iii) What is the contribution of the MSE strategy to poverty reduction and income change?

iv) What is the sustainability of the MSE strategy in terms of business development and growth?

v) What constraints and challenges are faced by the MSE strategy and the participants?

1.4. Methodology

A participatory and interactive research methodology involving different stakeholders has been adopted for the research. The stakeholders are the MSE operators, MSE strategy implementers, city and town managers and support service providers.

The methodology includes the use of secondary data (i.e., desk research) as well as field findings through questionnaires and interviews.

1.4.1. Study area

The study has been carried out in four secondary towns of Ethiopia, namely, Bahir Dar, Mekelle, Hawassa and Adama (see map 1). These towns form the capital cities of the four big Regions. The four secondary towns are selected purposively since the MSE strategy in urban areas is a national program and any effort towards its implementation will be highly visible in these towns. They are also towns with the highest concentration of MSEs. Findings from these secondary towns could therefore be used as lessons for other small and intermediate towns where such strategy is not as advanced as in the big towns.

1.4.2. Sampling method and sample size

The main purpose of the study is to understand the nature of MSE policy and the problems and successes of MSEs in poverty reduction, employment generation and business development. Program beneficiaries or MSE operators are one source of information. MSEs thus form the primary sampling unit. The samples were selected from the four secondary cities mentioned above. The total sample size for the study was 200 MSEs, with 50 MSEs selected from each city. The reason for using a fixed sample size from each city is to avoid the bias that may be generated if a disproportionate sampling size is adopted.

The selection strategy involved first obtaining a sampling frame. The sample frame was obtained from each city's micro- and small-scale enterprises agency. Those included in the sample frame are MSEs organized by the program as new

5

establishments and those which are already established but assisted by the program. The MSEs in urban areas were then stratified by the nature of their activities and forms of organization, i.e., whether cooperative or private. The samples were then selected randomly from each group proportionally. Operators were sampled from each of the MSEs depending on the number of operators. In those MSEs where the number of operators is four or below, all the members were interviewed. In those MSEs where the number of operators exceeded four, four operators were interviewed. The reason for selecting only four operators is to make the size of interviewees manageable given the limited time and cost of the study. A total of 557 operators were selected and included in this study in addition to the 200 business establishments.

1.4.3. Selection of key informants

Key informants were selected for an in-depth interview. The key informants were those individuals working in the implementing agencies both at city and kebele levels. Those responsible for the management of cities and involved in poverty reduction were used as key informants to understand the nature of their policy and strategy and the institutional arrangement.

1.4.4. Data collection

Desk review of documents
The desk review examined current government policies, plans and directives, which are relevant to MSE and urban development.

Structured Questionnaire
A structured questionnaire was prepared to collect data from the MSEs. The questionnaire   included information pertaining to the MSEs and operators' characteristics, financial and non-financial needs of MSE operators, problems and constraints in accessing services, among others. The survey questionnaire was pilot-tested in order to get feedback and improve upon it. The survey was carried out in a face-to-face manner through enumerators and supervisors between October and November 2009. Both were trained intensively on each question. While enumerators were engaged in actual data collection, supervisors provided guidance to the enumerators and checked errors on the spot.

Unstructured questionnaire
An unstructured questionnaire was used to collect data from key informants. The questionnaire sought information on the components of the strategy, the modalities of implementation, institutional arrangements, support provided,

nature of employment created, challenges and prospects of MSEs, etc. These were undertaken by principal researchers in all the study areas.

1.4.5. Data analysis

Data from the MSEs were analyzed using statistical packages. The data were presented using graphs and statistical summaries. The qualitative data were analyzed to help capture aspects of the research that could not be done through the quantitative method, on the one hand, and to triangulate research findings derived from the literature review and different secondary sources, such as reports, policy manuals and implementation directives, on the other hand.

1.5. Limitation of the Study

This study has used the four secondary cities as cases. These cases were selected purposively. The MSE strategy however is implemented in several secondary, small and big cities of the country. The conclusions emanating from the results, therefore, have to be taken cautiously since some of the results may not be generalizable to specific local conditions of other cities and towns. In achieving its objective, the study has relied on assessing the beneficiaries who are currently engaged in the MSE sector and receive assistance from the government. It will be interesting to compare beneficiaries and non-beneficiaries to fully capture the effects of the MSE strategy. Lastly, the study has also faced some problems in the field work. In particular there were data inconsistency between what is reported by the MSE sector offices and field data. Some of the enterprises registered and licensed by the agency are not operational or do not exist in the field. Such data inconsistency needs to be corrected by the MSE agency in the future.

Fig. 1: Map of the Study towns

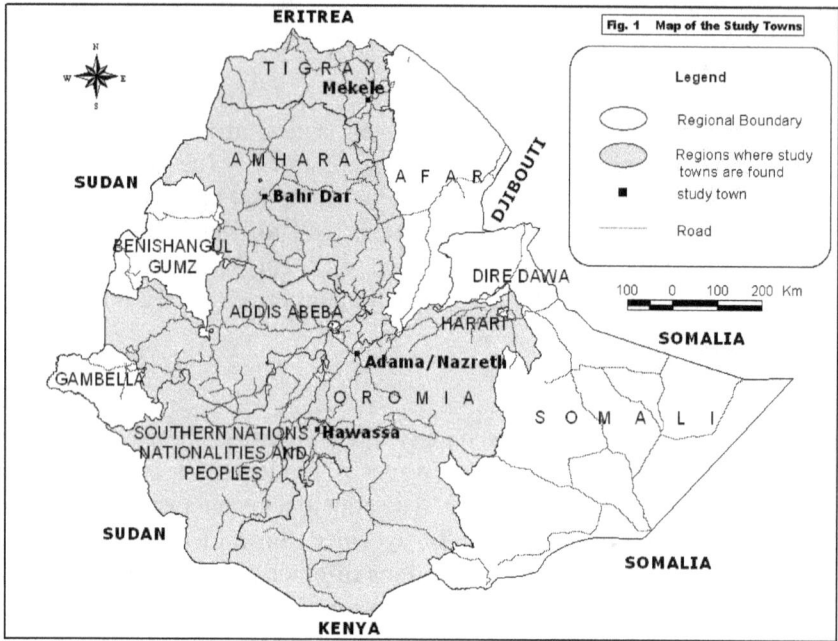

Fig. 1 Map of the Study Towns

2. Literature Review

2.1. The MSE Sector: Definition and Typologies

The terms 'micro-' 'small-scale' and 'medium', are often used to refer to different categories of micro- and small-business enterprises. These can be production, service or retail business entities. Generally, however, the distinction seems to connote the scale and size of these enterprises in terms of capital, labor absorption capacity, market share and other important criteria, such as operating revenue or annual or monthly turnover or growth performance. Often, such criteria are used to classify these businesses into different categories. For example, on the basis of past growth performance, enterprises are classified as new-starts, no growth firms, small growth firms and graduates (Harvie 2003). Other classification looks at enterprises from micro-finance perspectives.

Perhaps the most useful classification of enterprises with obvious policy implication is the one which distinguishes between livelihood (survival) activities or enterprises versus growth oriented or viable enterprises (Harvie

2003). These two types of enterprises have distinct characteristics with different policy implications. The livelihood (survival) enterprises are the ones in which the entrepreneur is pushed into. These are activities undertaken to support family income and they could be seasonal or part-time. They require no skill or require low skill and the entry barrier is minimal. As a result, they are highly overcrowded activities. Earnings from these activities are used to support survival and the enterprises have potential for making short term impact on poverty. The growth-oriented activities require skills restricting entry. Entrepreneurs are attracted to the growth-oriented activities by consideration of profits and out of choice. Surplus is re-invested and they form the basis for growth and sustainable development (Harvie 2003). Table 1 provides a summary of the basic differences between the two types of enterprises. This classification conforms with the perspective that views entry to micro-enterprises as being driven by poverty or by entrepreneurial spirit.

Table 2.1. Differences between livelihood and growth-oriented enterprises

Elements	Livelihood enterprises	Growth oriented enterprises
1. Capitalization	Relatively low	Higher, but initial capital is usually similar
2. Education (entrepreneur)	Little formal education	Usually at least secondary schooling
3. Skills and experience	Relatively low, except for skills acquired traditionally as in handicrafts; trading often a fertile training ground for latter manufacturing of the same product	Higher, more often acquired through vocational training and or previous wage employment
4. Gender	High (often) participation of women	Lower participation of women but still high in some cultures
5. Sector	High proportion in livestock, backyard poultry, food processing and petty trading	High proportion in manufacturing and services requiring services

Table 2.1. *Cont'd.*

Elements	Livelihood enterprises	Growth oriented enterprises
6. Competition	Usually function in perfect competitive market with low barriers to entry and little scope for cutting costs by intensive use of family labor and even by offering credit	Often occupy 'niche' market with more scope for specialization and product differentiation
7. Seasonality	Often seasonal and tied to crop cycle, school year, major festivals	Less affected by seasonality, and function throughout the year even if at varying levels
8. Contribution to household income	Usually a secondary source (although vital)	Usually the only enterprise
9. Whether only enterprise	Usually one of several multiple enterprises (to compensate for seasonality and low returns)	Usually the only enterprise
10. Use of hired labor	Infrequent, mostly use family labor	More common, often use relatives or children
11. Surpluses and re-investment	Surpluses limited and often ploughed back into household expenditure	Reinvestment of surpluses the norm
12. Use of credit	Trading activities often started on a consignment basis, livestock required on a profit sharing basis, boats and rickshaw on lease, however, in order to compete, often become net lender especially in trading and restaurants	Credit available from a wider range (informal and semi formal) and a greater two-way flow of credit so that micro-enterprises are more often net lenders than livelihood enterprises
13. Potential for growth	Limited in terms of new employment generation, but offer scope for increases in sale, productivity, profitability and income; growth blocked often by demand constraints; resource constraints and physical constraints (space in home and yard)	Have growth potential; number of workers higher, with more paid employees; employment usually of higher quality

SOURCE: Asian Development Bank (1997) cited in Harvie.

Notwithstanding the above classification, different countries use different criteria to distinguish these business enterprises from other economic entities within their national territory. What is common in many situations (including Ethiopia), however, is that policies and programs for MSE development fall principally under the portfolio of the ministry of industry and commerce or the equivalent. The following are sample definitions and characteristics of MSEs taken from randomly selected countries (Table 2).

Table 2 shows that different countries have different definitions and categorizations of MSEs. In summary, there is no single or universally acceptable definition on which there is complete consensus. This makes the practice of counting the number of MSEs and measuring their impact extremely difficult across countries.

Table 2.2. Definition of MSEs by different countries and agencies

Country	Definition
Botswana	In 1998, the Small, Medium and Micro-Enterprise Task Force developed definitions for the three categories of business enterprises as follows: (a) Micro-enterprises: an enterprise which has less than six workers including the owner and an annual turnover of less than P. 60,000; (b) Small enterprise: an enterprise which employs less than 25 paid employees, and has an annual turnover of between P. 60,000 and P. 1,500,000; Medium-sized enterprise: employs less than 100 paid employees and has an annual turnover of between P.1,500,000 and P.8,000,000 (http: www.scialert.net/2002.563.569=PDF.
Burkina Faso	According to the Ministry of Commerce, Industry and Crafts (MCIA), an MSE is classified as any private enterprise (owned by, or formed in, association with a citizen of Burkina Faso) which is legally incorporated and complies with the following conditions: (i) the manager is the owner or a partner; (ii) the enterprise maintains accounts in keeping with prescribed principles; (iii) has a total investment of 5 -200 million CFA; and (iv) has a minimum number of three salaried employees registered with the National Social Security (INSD 1993).
Zambia	The Small Enterprises Act of 1996 defines SMEs as follows: *Micro-*: an enterprise with total investment excluding land and building that does not exceed 50 million Zambian Kwacha; annual turnover that does not exceed 20 million Zambian Kwacha and employing up to 10 persons. *Small*: an enterprise whose total investment excluding land and buildings does not exceed 50 million Kwacha in case of manufacturing and processing enterprise and 10 million Kwacha in case of a trading and services enterprises; and an annual turnover that does not exceed 80 million Zambian Kwacha and employing up to 30 people. The act does not provide a definition for medium-size enterprises (Chibwe 2008).

Table 2.2. *Cont'd.*

Country	Definition
Indonesia	In Indonesia, a small enterprise is defined as an enterprise (i) with asset not including land and buildings less than RP. 200 million, or (ii) with annual sales volume not more than RP. 1 million, (iii) owned by an Indonesian citizen, (iv) independent and not affiliated with bigger enterprises; and (v) can be individual business with or without legal license including cooperatives. Medium enterprises are defined as a business entity with total asset bigger than that of small enterprises, but less than RP. 10 billion. On the other hand, micro- enterprises are not yet formally defined and only for statistical purposes, they are defined as economic entities with sales volume less than RP.50 million (Dipta 2004).
Nepal	An official definition of medium-sized enterprises does not exist. Nevertheless, the country classifies its industrial enterprises according to four categories: cottage, small, medium-sized and large, based on their level of fixed capital investment. The Industrial Enterprises Act of 1992 classifies cottage industries as traditional industries that utilize specific skills or raw materials and resources, which are labor intensive and are related to national tradition, art and culture. Industries with a fixed capital investment of up to 10 million Nepalese rupees are classified as small industries. Enterprises with a fixed capital investment of between 10 and 50 million Nepalese rupees are classified as medium-sized, and those with a fixed capital investment of more than 50 million Nepalese rupees are categorized as large.
The European Union	The European Union recognizes three types of small enterprises: micro, small and medium sized. Each of these has differing employee, turnover and asset criteria. These three-size groups of non-subsidiary independent businesses make up what are termed as small and medium sized enterprises (SMEs). Accordingly, micro--enterprises employ less than 10 people and have a turnover of less than 2 million Euros. Small enterprises have employees of less than 50 and a turnover of less than 10 million Euros; and, medium-sized enterprises employ less than 250 people and have a turnover of less than 50 million Euros (Carter and Jones-Evans 2004).
The World Bank	The World Bank classifies SMEs into different categories in terms of number of employees, extent of total asset and estimated amount of annual turnover. According to these criteria, 2 of the 3 characteristics must be met for an enterprise to be classified in a particular category. Hence, a micro-enterprise employs between 1-10 people, must have less than $100,000 in total assets, and an annual turnover of less than $100,000. A small enterprise employs 11-50 people, must have total asset of between $100,000-3,000,000, and an annual turnover of $1000,000-3,000,000; and medium enterprise employs between 51-300 people, must have total assets of between $3,000,000-15,000,000 million, and an annual turnover of $3,000,000-15,000,000million(http://www.ec.europa.eu/enterprise,enterprisepolicy,sme definition/sme user guide).

Table 2.2. *Cont'd.*

Country	Definition
Ethiopia	Currently, two definitions are being used to classify MSEs in Ethiopia: One by the Ministry of Trade and Industry (MoTI) and another one by the Central Statistical Agency. According to MoTI, micro-enterprises are those businesses firms in the formal and informal sector with a paid up capital not exceeding Birr 20,000.00 and excluding high consultancy firms and other high tech establishments. On the other hand, small enterprises are those businesses with a paid up capital above Birr 20,000.00 but not exceeding Birr 500,000 and excluding high tech consultancy firms and other high-tech establishments (FDRE 1997).

Alternatively, the Central Statistical Agency (CSA) employs the following categories for the purpose of compiling statistical information on MSEs:

(a)   Establishments employing less than ten persons and using motor operated equipment are considered as small-scale manufacturing enterprises;

(b)   Enterprises in the micro-enterprise category are subdivided into informal sector operations and cottage and handicraft industries:

    (i)   Cottage and handicraft industries are those establishments performing their activities by using non-power driven machines;

    (ii)   The informal sector is defined as household type establishments or activities which are non-registered companies or cooperatives operating with less than 10 persons (CSA 1999b; 2000).

2.2. MSEs, Economic Growth and Employment

There are three basic arguments for pro-SME policy (Beck, Demirguc-kunt and Lenvine 2003). First, MSEs enhance competition and entrepreneurship. This results in economy-wide external benefits in efficiency, innovation and aggregate productivity.   Second, MSEs are considered to be generally more productive than large firms though MSE development is impeded with financial and institutional failures. Third, MSE expansion boosts employment more than large firm growth because MSEs are more labor intensive. The last argument is directly related to poverty reduction (see below).

Despite the above pro-SMEs argument, there are skeptics who mention that SMEs are not better than large firms and in fact the benefit of large firms outweigh that of small firms in a number of ways. In particular, in relation to employment, the argument is that large firms offer more stable employment, higher wages and more non-wage benefits than small firms in developed and developing countries (Brown et al. and Rosenywig cited in Beck, Demirguc-kunt and Lenvine 2003). In short, the argument emphasizes that SMEs are not necessarily more suitable to the labor abundance and capital shortage characteristics of developing countries.

There are several empirical studies that attempted to unravel the role of MSEs in employment growth and fostering economic dynamism. For example, Menash, Tribe, and Weiss (2007) studied the relation between firm characteristics and economic performance and the extent of economic dynamism in the small-scale industrial sector. Regarding the latter, the issue is whether the small-scale enterprises are sources of dynamism or simply a means of generating subsistence income. Using a survey data from the Central Region in Ghana, the authors found out that out of the studied firms, 55% recorded an increase in their labor force, 32% showed no change, and 13% showed a decline. The average increase was significantly higher for small firms as compared to micro- and very small firms. The implication is that small-scale industrial firms are capable of generating employment growth. It was also found out that the substantial amount of work in both rural and urban areas is of part-time nature.

2.3. MSEs and Poverty Reduction

Micro- and small enterprise (MSE) development is one of the enduring approaches of poverty reduction. The idea emerged in the 1980s as a result of interest in the informal sector. It is a meeting point between the neo-liberal interest to promote private enterprise and the market as creator and distributor of resources and grassroots practitioners' focus on the on-the ground problem of poverty recognizing local people's own agency (Evesole 2004). Micro-enterprise development provides a perfect opportunity for self-help development as poor people in developing countries are observed to create wealth and employ themselves. The approach looks at the poor people as entrepreneurs. As a result, development interventions at various levels embraced micro-enterprises as the key to unlocking the potential of stagnant economies and improving the livelihoods of the poor (ibid). For example, between 1989-2003, the World Bank approved more than $10 billion in support programs including $1.5 billion in 2002 (Beck, Demirguc-kunt and Lenvine 2003). Most community development programs world wide now include an enterprise component.

The MSEs, by expanding entrepreneurship, provide employment and thus sustainable income. They also provide lower-level goods and services for the poor people. The profits from MSEs also stay locally creating flow-on benefits to disadvantaged areas. Thus, the benefits from micro-enterprises accrue to poor individuals, families and communities. With regard to the latter, MSEs are known for revitalizing depressed neighborhoods and communities (Nelson 2000).

Some empirical studies find a positive role of MSEs in poverty reduction. Thapa (2007) studied the relationship between household income and engagement in micro-enterprises in Nepal. Using methods of quasi-experimental design and comparing experimental and control groups, he found out that engagement in micro-enterprises was found to have a positive impact on increasing household income. The author recommended that government should focus on developing policies to extend micro-enterprises together with raising educational levels

Nepal has a micro-enterprise development program (MEDEP) for poverty reduction. The program started in 1998 by the Nepal Government with technical and financial support from UNDP in ten poor districts (Shrestha n.d.). The MEDEP is a demand-driven program. The aim is to create employment and income opportunities to bring about sustainable livelihood of the poor. The specific goals are poverty reduction of low-income families, capacity building of service delivery organizations, and policy recommendation to the government. The main targets were low income families, unemployed youth and unemployed men and women, self-employed proprietors and micro-enterprise owners. The program is expressed as a success. The success of the program is due to its demand-driven and integrated approaches, the systematic processes and the attention it accorded to gender and sustainability (ibid)

In terms of the demand-driven approach, program activities are located according to the needs and demands of the market and the ability and potential of micro-entrepreneurs to meet those demands. Thus resource potential, people and market demand for products and services are considered in selecting program activities. The systemic process of the MEDEP starts with analysis of the socio-economic, area potential and market survey. The analysis looks at people, resources and market. The integrated approach of the program seeks to provide a package of services to entrepreneurs depending on their needs. The package includes appropriate technology, information, training, marketing, micro-finance and social mobilization. The gender component examines gender specific considerations to addresses the issue of gender inequality. Sustainability is an important criteria and it included three components. These are demand-driven, capacity building, and sustainable enterprise partnership. Activities in the program focus on building the capacity of local businesses, institutions and organizations to promote micro-enterprises. The program also promoted strategic alliance and networks between program partners to support micro-enterprise development. The program had impacts on increasing income, improving local economy, reducing poverty, empowering women, and creating a micro-macro linkage.

Despite the positive role MSEs play in poverty reduction, some skepticism is expressed as regards their viability and sustainability. For example, in USA, some scholars have identified that the strategy fails to reach the poor as most studies show that most participants are fairly educated individuals who can be employed in the formal wage sector (Schreiner and Woller 2003).

2.4. MSE Promotional Programs

Different types of MSEs have different objectives and they also entail different promotional programs. The kinds of assistance that are required for enterprise development are numerous. In general terms, they could be divided into financial and non-financial services. Finance is a critical input for MSE growth and expansion. Despite this, however, very few firms actually borrow capital. In the small towns of the Amhara Region in Ethiopia, for example, a study found out that only 13.6% of the enterprises borrow from different sources (Tegegne and Mulat 2005). Availability of capital for loan, loan requirements, use of own resources, lack of interest among financial institutions to finance MSEs could be some of the problems for limited MSE operators to engage in micro-enterprise credit. In terms of lack of interest to finance MSEs, commercial banks are notable (Wolday 2002). Banks will not be interested to finance MSEs because MSEs are believed to have high risks and transaction costs which may be perceived or real (Wolday 2002). This is also compounded by supervisory and capital adequacy requirements that penalize banks for lending to enterprises that lack traditional collateral (Wolday 2002). Even if banks are willing to finance MSEs, their limited availability and coverage and their high collateral requirement in Ethiopia will pose difficulty to widely reach the MSEs sector.

There is a general observation that emphasis on credit should not be allowed to neglect factors such as marketing or technology assistance which may be critical to the success and failure of micro- and small enterprises (Harper cited in Wolday 2002). The term business development service (BDS) is used to include a wide variety of non-financial services: labor and management training; extension, consultancy and counseling; marketing and information services; technology development and diffusion; mechanisms to improve business linkages, sub-contracting; franchising and business clusters. The new approach in the provision of BDS is emphasis on demand and the creation of BDS that is more vibrant and reaches a large number of MSEs (Wolday 2002). In the new approach, government and donors are expected to pay facilitating roles in both the supply and demand sides. On the supply side, the facilitators can provide support to BDS providers to develop new service products, promote good practices, build the capacity of BDS providers while on the demand side they can educate MSE operators on the potential benefits of BDS, and promote better policy environment for BDS operators (Wolday 2002).

The foregoing highlights that while micro- and small-scale enterprise approach is an accepted wisdom to reduce poverty and generate employment, there is a need to address issues that may circumvent the approach. The target beneficiaries and their needs, the types of activities, the kinds of support provided, the level of earnings, the local context, the nature of planning for micro-enterprises, the changes brought about by MSEs, the complementarity of the approach to other poverty reduction strategy and the sustainability of the approach are some of the issues that need to be clarified in assessing an MSE strategy. The present study addresses some of these issues.

3. The Urban Micro- and Small Enterprises Strategy and Its Implementation in the Study Towns and Regions

As has been indicated earlier, the root policy for MSE strategy implementation in the study towns and cities is the urban development and industry package. Urban development in Ethiopia got attention following the onset of the Poverty Reduction Strategic Program (PRSP) document by the Government. This was followed by the Plan for Accelerated and Sustainable Development to End Poverty (PASDEP). The latter encapsulated the urban development policy as a major component to address the problem of urban areas in the country's overall growth strategy (Tegegne 2007). In terms of urban development, the strategy indicates that there is a need to focus on urban poverty and welfare as much as on enhancing the contribution of urban centers for national development (MoFED 2006). The national urban development policy has two main packages: the urban development package and the urban good governance package.

The urban development package has a number of inter-related objectives, including reducing unemployment and poverty; improving the capacity of the construction industry; alleviating the existing housing problems; promoting urban areas as engines of economic growth and improving urban social and economic infrastructure, particularly for the youth (Tegegne 2007). The package has five pillars: micro/small enterprise development program, integrated housing development program, youth development program, provision of land, infrastructure, services and facilities, and rural-urban and urban-urban linkages. It also has eight goals which are related to the five pillars (Table 3.1).

The MSE program of the national urban development policy aims at creating opportunities for 1.5 million residents through establishment of one-stop service centers, MSE extension workers, provision of premise and loan, business development services, promoting market opportunities and market linkages and equipping enterprises with modern equipment and machineries (MoWUD 2007). The 1.5 million beneficiaries will be the existing MSE operators/entrepreneurs, MSE operators/entrepreneurs involved in the integrated housing development program, new technical vocational and educational training program graduates and the unemployed youth (MoWUD 2007).

Table 3.1. Goals of the urban development package

Goal	Target
Goal 1	Construct 400,000 houses in 72 urban centers from EFY 2006/07 to 2009/10. Twenty to thirty percent of the beneficiaries will be women
Goal 2	Create employment opportunities for 1.5 million urban residents in 825 urban centers during EFY 2006/07-2009/10. Fifty percent of the beneficiaries will be women
Goal 3	Enable the voluntary creation of 100,000 small enterprises on a sustainable bases in the construction industry
Goal 4	Provide social facilities (8,250 classrooms, 1030 libraries, 503 youth centers, 7,236 football fields, and 503 hand/basketball fields) for youth to gain knowledge and engage in recreation in a productive and meaningful way. Fifty percent of benefiting youths will be girls
Goal 5	Ensure the participation of urban residents, public authorities and other stakeholders in all programs
Goal 6	Secure funds that provide for a total investment during EFY 2006/07 to 2009/10 of EB 23.3 billion. EB 15.8 billion for the integrated housing development program, Ethiopian Birr (EB) 6.2 billion for the micro- and small enterprise development program and EB 1.3 for the Youth program.
Goal 7	Ensure delivery of a total of 13,825 hectares of serviced land in all urban centers: 1,700 hectares to support the integrated housing development program (IHDP); 4,900 hectares for micro- and small enterprise development; 1425 hectares for youth development program; and 5,800 hectares for other development
Goal 8	Secure funds for the EFY 2006/07 budget in foreign currency equivalent to USD 73.9 million

SOURCE: Urban PASDEP, unpublished.

Besides the above national initiative on urban development and a focus on MSEs, each Region has some MSE policy initiative. For example, the Southern Region had a 10 year plan on MSE development beginning from 1995/96 EC with a goal of covering 420,000 individuals. A five-member team consisting of the Bureau of Industry, the Omo micro-finance, housing agency, TVET and the private sector is also established to spearhead the MSE development program.

The field study showed that in all Regions, MSE development is undertaken both in large cities and small towns. As a result, the number of MSEs has grown significantly in different Regions. For example, in Tigray Region, the total number of MSEs was 44,000 in the year 2007, 74447 in the year 2008 and 100,000 in the year 2009. In the year 2009, out of the 100,000 MSEs, 4000 were cooperatives. In Hawassa city alone, there were 18,000 MSE members and 1,100 cooperatives in the year 2009. Out of the 18,000 members, 12,000 were involved in the package program while the remaining 6000 were found in the regular program.

In the four Regions where the study towns are found, 71,568 enterprises were created and these generated 395,806 employment opportunities in the year 2009 (Table 3.2).

Table 3.2. Number of enterprises and employment created in 2009

Regions	Number of MSE enterprises created	Number of employment created
Tigray	1255	48423
Amhara	55876	136114
Oromia	9827	179031
SNNPR	4610	32238
Total	**71568**	**395806**

SOURCE: Ministry of Urban development and Housing.

The implementation of the MSE program in different Regions involves forging institutional structure, organizing modalities and providing support services.

3.1. Institutional Structure

Different Regions have developed different institutional structures to implement the MSE strategy. In Amhara Region, there are Regional, zonal, city and kebele offices. Within the city, one-stop centers are also established. They serve one or two kebeles depending on the situation. In Bahir Dar, for example, there are nine kebeles and six one-stop centers. Each one-stop center is staffed with three people: a coordinator, registration and licensing officer, and land facilitation officer.

In Tigray, MSE development is undertaken in the major cities and woreda towns. The major cities are twelve and the woreda towns are 34 in number. The major cities have sub-cities and kebeles. In Mekelle, for example, which is one of the major cities, there are seven sub-cities and each has its own trade and industry office and one-stop center. At sub-city level, there are eight employees. Three of them are feasibility experts, two are generalists and the remaining three are representatives (micro-finance and cooperative) and a coordinator. In the remaining 11 cities there are similar arrangements. All the cities have micro-finance and cooperative representatives. The cities, depending on the local condition and local need, however, employ specialists such as an urban agriculture expert, a mechanical engineer or other expert. One stop-centers are found at city level in woreda towns. Since 2007, extension workers were also assigned. At the beginning, there were only 2 extension workers in every kebele. Recently, after the implementation of the business process re-engineering (BPR) reform, there is one extension worker for every 500 MSEs. The extension workers are politically accountable to kebele administrations but are technically accountable to the one-stop center.

In the SNNPR, the micro- and enterprise agency is found at Regional, zonal, city and kebele levels. There are 22 big cities, 45 sub-cities, and 89 woreda towns. At Regional level, there are 20 employees (professionals) who are further designated as generalists and technologists. At zonal levels, there are 3-5 professionals; at woreda level, there are 3 professionals; at sub-city level, there are 12 professionals. These 12 professionals are further classified as agents (these are specialists in the four areas of metal work, construction, textile and agricultural processing), facilitators and support staff.

Currently, the MSE strategy has assumed a central position and has received political support in all Regions. For example, in Tigray, the MSE program is a core process. As a core process, it is mainly concerned with promotion and expansion of the MSEs. The head of the core process is expected to spend 70% of his (her) time on promotion and expansion of MSEs. It was also indicated that the MSE program has political support and leadership. It thus has become a major priority area in the Region and is followed closely by political leaders.

3.2. Modalities of Organizing MSE Activities

In general, beneficiaries who are recruited for MSE operation should be residents of the city, unemployed and possess some knowledge or experience in the field they want to engage in. In many cases these individuals form associations. There are different ways of forming MSE association in different Regions. These include:

i) The office organizes the unemployed by following appropriate procedures;

ii) TVET graduates form associations on their own; and

iii) Different offices (women's office, youth offices, etc.) organize people and send them to Micro- and small enterprises agencies.

There are instances in which some people are left unrecruited despite their interest to form associations. This is due to capacity problems.

In Tigray, operators choose the modalities of engaging in the MSE activity. They can engage as cooperatives, private owners or private limited companies (PLCs). Cooperatives are exempted from taxes as long as individual members do not receive dividends. In the Southern Region, there is a transition period of two years during which time MSEs are made to stay as micro-business ventures. During these two years, it is believed that the MSEs will be able to create wealth, generate enough saving and establish synergy among members. This will give them a strong economic foundation. After the end of the two years, MSEs can follow either the cooperative mode or the private business route, such as a PLC. Besides, in the Southern Region, MSEs are classified as package and regular programs. Those under the package programs are usually cooperatives and involve in sectors designated as 'growth-oriented sectors'. Those under regular programs could include existing MSEs and those who are mainly involved in service provision, such as retailing, small hotels, etc. The MSEs under the package program receive a great variety of assistance (13 in number) while those in the regular program receive less number of services (3 in number). The same is true in Adama city.

3.3. Support Services

The range of assistance offered to the MSEs are similar across cities. These are credit, working premise, training, market linkage, business development services (BDSs), information, etc. Besides these range of services, Tigray provides incubation center as well, i.e., provision of basic facilities, such as telephone, furniture, etc., until the businesses take off.

3.4. Credit

Credit is usually given by micro-finance institutions. The Regional government or the city administration facilitates by providing a revolving fund[1] or acting as collateral for MSEs. Dedebit Micro-finance, Amhara Credit and Saving Institution (ACSI), Oromia Micro-finance and Omo Micro-finance are the main financing agencies in Tigray, Amhara, Oromia and the Southern Regions, respectively. Cooperatives are the main beneficiaries of government-mediated loan and credit services. All Regions have reported high repayment rates. For example, the repayment rate in Hawassa town is 90%.

Regions charge different interest rates for the micro-credit provided. In Hawassa, the Omo Micro-finance charges 10% interest rate, which is much

---

[1] According to the Bureau of Industry of the Southern region, the regional government has provided 97 million birr to Omo Micro-finance as revolving fund.

lower than the interest rate charged by ASCI or Dedebit. A lower interest rate is advantageous to micro-businesses. Since micro-businesses work at the margins, high interest rates can easily devour the already meager profits of borrowers. The challenge is how to provide funds for micro-businesses at an interest rate that is affordable while at the same time beneficial to lenders (Salmon 2004).

The amount of loan disbursed at Regional level for the year 2009 indicates that in the Regions where the four secondary towns are found a total of 423 million Birr was disbursed. Tigray and Amhara each had about 30,000 loan beneficiaries (Table 3.3).

Table 3.3. Amount of loan disbursed and number of beneficiaries, 2009 (Mn Birr)

Regions	Loan disbursed	Number of beneficiaries
Tigray	110.0	29521
Amhara	110.3	29882
Oromia	67.3	18453
SNNPR	135.4	-

SOURCE: Ministry of Urban Development and Housing.

The amount of loan provided to MSEs varies depending on the nature of the sector. For example, informants in Hawassa city revealed that in the Southern Region MSEs, which need to purchase machinery, qualify for a loan of 260,000 Birr; those working in producing pre-cast beam qualify for a loan of 270,000 Birr; and those engaged in metal work are given a loan of 60,000 Birr. Recently, however, particularly after the implementation of the business process re-engineering (BPR), the loan amount is decided on the basis of the business plan each MSE prepares[2]. The business plan is reviewed by committees at sub-city and city levels.

There is a high level of backlog of enterprises demanding credit in all Regions. This is evidenced in Adama, Hawassa and Bahir Dar. For example, in Hawassa city, loan requests equivalent to about 15 million Birr are deferred to the 2009/10 fiscal year from the previous year. This is a clear indication of a mismatch between supply and demand for credit.

3.5 Working Premise

Until recently, MSEs in all cities were provided land by the municipality to be used as working space. For example, the Hawassa municipality had allocated

---

[2] Individuals operating MSEs qualify for a loan of 5000 birr.

about 230,000 sq. meters of land to beneficiaries by the year 2009. At Regional levels, huge amounts of land have been allotted to MSEs (Table 3.4). Lately, it was observed that the provision of land had put high pressure on the land resource of the cities.

Table 3.4. Land prepared and shades constructed for MSEs

Region	Land prepared (m2)	Number of beneficiaries from land	Number of shades constructible
Tigray	-	-	207
Amhara	5,621,806	74,000	1,296
Oromia	1,714,114	269,817	735
SNNPR	328,680	-	-

SOURCE: Ministry of Urban Development and Housing.

There is now a shift from providing land for MSEs to providing premises for rent. While such a strategy is useful to alleviate the pressure on land, which is the major constraint in all towns, it has its own financial implication. Among other things, a huge amount of money is required to construct production and marketing premises for rent. In Tigray, for example, in 2008, about 52 million Birr was allocated to construct production and marketing centers in 38 cities. Of this, the Regional government allotted 22 million and the cities contributed 30 million Birr. In 2009, the Regional government allotted 20 million Birr and the cities allotted 30 million Birr for the construction of production and marketing centers (interview with the head of Micro- enterprise core process). In the Southern Region, a huge resource is allotted for the construction of clusters. The Regional government covered 40% of the cost for cluster development while 60% is covered by cities.

3.6. Training

In all study cities, two types of training are provided to MSEs: technical and business training. Extension workers provide business training while Regional or city TVET colleges provide technical training. Other bodies are also involved in training. In particular, in Amhara Region, there are community skill training centers which provide training in leather making, weaving, knitting and carpentry. There are also a few private MSEs which provide training on cost-sharing basis. Table 3.5 shows the number of trainees in the year 2009 in the four Regions.

Table 3.5. Number of trainees in MSE sector

Region	Number of trainees
Tigray	60,000
Amhara	91,292
Oromia	76.345
SNNPR	96,504

SOURCE: Ministry of Urban Development and Housing.

The duration of training varies depending on the type of training. In Amhara Region, training in cobble stone work is given for 15 days while training in tailoring is given for one month. Business training is of shorter duration and is usually given for 3or 4 days.

It is not clear how these short trainings impart the necessary skills for the trainees. In general, however, it is difficult to transfer human capital in short courses (Shreiner 2001). It is not also clear how trainings are tailored to the needs of the adult trainees. In fact, a key informant in the Amhara Region commented that institutions such as TVET lack entrepreneurial experience and as a result their training is focused more on theory rather than practice – a serious concern about the relevance and quality of training provided.

3.7 Market Linkage

Market linkage is an attempt to create demand for MSE products so that they can sustain their operation. The major form of market linkage is to link MSEs with government institutions and projects. As a result, MSEs are linked with condominium house construction projects, universities, prisons, hospitals etc. These government institutions contract out some of their activities to the MSEs. For instance, MSEs provide food for universities and prisons. MSEs also provide the main construction inputs, such as pre-cast beam, hollow blocks, for government condominium houses.

Other efforts under market linkage include organizing bazaars and trade fairs in cities and towns. This is basically meant to popularize the products of MSEs.

Many Regions have developed regulations that allow the MSEs to bid and take a contract from government institutions. The Southern Region has enacted a regulation that demands all bids up to 300,000 Birr be given to the MSEs. The MSEs can bid up to 300,000 Birr each time. Each MSE can bid for three times only up to a total of 900,000 Birr. In Amhara, the MSEs. particularly cooperative MSEs, are allowed to compete without CPOs and are given 13 points bonus when competing with others. MSEs can also bid for up to one million Birr without producing proof for value added tax (VAT) registration. In Tigray, construction MSEs are allowed to take contract of up to 500,000 Birr and clothing and textile MSEs are allowed to take contract of up to 100,000 Birr. Table 3.6 shows the number of enterprises who enjoyed market linkages and the estimated value of market linkages. It can be seen that many enterprises are beneficiaries of market linkage, which has a significant value.

Table 3.6. Number of enterprises enjoying market linkages

Region	Number of enterprises benefiting from market linkages	Estimated value of market linkages (million Birr)
Tigray	27623	681
Amhara	36607	157
Oromia	26	-
SNNPR	31675	-

SOURCE: Ministry of Urban Development and Housing.

3.8. Business Development Services (BDSs)

BDS are provided by extension agents. In Amhara Region, one extension agent provides services for 15-20 operators. The extension agents prepare business profiles and address the needs of the businesses accordingly. In Tigray, one extension worker is expected to provide BDS support for 5 months to 10-15 MSEs. The extension worker regularly monitors the MSEs. It provides advice to each MSE twice a week.

3.9. Access to Support Services

Though in principle different support services are provided for MSEs, not all of them get the services equally and nor is equal attention given to all MSEs. Different distinctions are made among different MSEs in different Regions.

First, there is a distinction between the regular program and the package program. The former involves limited support services while the latter has an extensive service coverage. For example, in the Southern Region, it was indicated that the former has only 3 types of support services while the latter includes support services that number up to thirteen.

In general, MSEs which are classified as growth sectors are recipients of the full package. These growth sectors are those nationally identified sectors which are believed to add value in the production sectors. The six sectors are construction, wood and metal work, food preparation, textile, urban agriculture and municipal. MSEs not involved in growth sectors are recipients of limited service types. These MSEs include those which are involved in retailing and other service provision activities. In actual fact, these in general tend to be existing MSEs though some existing MSEs can also operate in the growth sectors. In general those MSEs operating under growth sectors operate in cooperative form and are mostly newly established MSEs. In Tigray, it was mentioned that the newly formed MSEs received full support since there is a need to strengthen them while the existing ones receive limited support as they have developed some capacity on their own. In Tigray, the main priority area for support is the construction sector. Following this, other priority sectors (textile, urban agriculture, metal and woodwork, municipal services, etc.) are chosen depending on the local condition of cities and woredas.

In Tigray, there is an elaborate system of accessing the different kinds of support the system provides. The extension workers first prepare MSE profiles for each business venture. This generates knowledge on what each MSE has and what assistance it needs. A committee composed of representatives from the women association, youth association, representatives from administration and the extension worker at sub-city level studies the enterprises to be supported. The extension worker suggests the MSEs to be supported and the kind of service. The committee then decides on the MSEs to be supported.

3.10. Graduation

The ultimate aim of the service provided to MSEs is to help them graduate and join the investment sector. There is a general agreement that MSEs are said to graduate once they reach the 500,000 Birr capital limit. After graduation, successful MSEs will be linked to the investment core process and the assistance they used to receive will be discontinued. The MSEs, in their attempt to maximize the support services, however, prefer to stay in the sector and tend not to disclose their actual capital for monitoring purposes.

It seems that there is no elaborate plan to promote the graduation of MSEs in all the study cities. The Southern Region, however, has specified a time frame within which MSEs need to graduate or risk the danger of not receiving support. The support provided for almost all the services in the MSEs in the Southern Region is only for four years. During these years, the MSEs should accumulate enough capital and experience that would allow them to graduate. Land provision in the Region, however, can extend up to the fifth year, one year more after other kinds of assistance have expired. The reason is to provide the MSEs with a grace period of one year since it is not easy to get own production site.

In Tigray, there is no time limit. This implies that MSEs can graduate in two years or may not graduate after 4 years. Upon graduation, these businesses are expected to compete in the national market on their own. This could be very difficult since most of them currently operate because they have a ready-made market or are protected from fierce competition as is done in the Amhara Region. The number of MSEs that have graduated from each Region so far is very limited. In Hawassa, it was found that there were only 7 MSE cooperatives which have graduated so far.

4. Micro- and Small Enterprises' and Operators' Characteristics in the Study Cities

4.1. Business Characteristics

4.1.1. Business typology, business lines and gender composition

For the purpose of providing organizational, technical and financial assistance, the MSE sector has been divided into 2 business typologies[3]: (a) Packages; and (b) Regular business enterprises. Package businesses are those organized and helped by MSE sector offices with organizers, credit, training, market and production space, licensing and regulation. In some Regions, these businesses are characterized as 'value adding' ventures because of the fact that most of them are either in the production or service line of business. In addition, it was learnt from field findings that they were often organized as cooperative undertakings rather than individual, partnership or group-owned business firms. Based on field discussions, it was also observed that Regional MSE sector offices/bureaus were more inclined towards giving greater technical and organizational support to these types of enterprises.

On the other hand, regular business enterprises are those that are already set up by an individual entrepreneur or partnerships or a group of entrepreneurs set

---

[3] Note that this is not true in all Regions. In some Regions, MSEs are recognized as cooperatives and individual business.

up as private limited companies. These receive either only partial or selectively available support from MSE offices/sector bureaus; and most often, are considered second priority areas of intervention. In many cases, most of these businesses would be considered for financial or organizational assistance only if they satisfy more stringent conditions (e.g., hefty collateral) than would be required of package enterprises.

As was indicated earlier, a total of 200 business firms were randomly selected for the study. Field findings indicated that out of these, 123 (61.5%) were under package programs and 77 (38.5%) were regular businesses. In the two categories, 64.9% and 35.1% of the respondents were males and females, respectively (Table 4.1).

Table 4.1. Gender breakdown of respondents, by business type

Gender	Type of business		%age
	Package	Regular	
Male	195	88	64.9
Female	81	72	35.1
Total	**276**	**160**	**100**

SOURCE: Field data.

In terms of gender breakdown by business type, it can be observed in Table 4.1 above that out of those questioned, men constituted 70.6% in the package businesses category whereas the proportion of women owners and operators was only 29.4%. In the regular business category, men operators and owners constituted 55% and women constituted 45% of the respondents. In both cases, it appears that male respondents have been the majority out of the sample.

As per the Micro- and Small Enterprises Development Strategy, there are seven lines of business in which MSE operators and owners can be engaged. These include food and food products; metal and wood work; textile and clothing; construction; urban agriculture; petty trade; and municipal services.

Based on a sample of 50 enterprises in each city, it was found that certain lines of business attracted more MSE operators and owners than others. It can be observed that petty trade (25.5%), construction (20.0%) and metal and wood work (18.5%) are the most popular lines of business, at least in terms of number of operators and owners (Table 4.2).

Together, the 3 lines of businesses command 64% of the total number of operators and owners sampled for the study. The least popular with relatively few owners and operators appears to be solid waste (2.5%), urban agriculture (10.0%), followed by textile and clothing, only with a slight lead (10.5%).

Engagements in the different lines of business activity tend to show gender difference (Table 4.3). The table shows that more female representation is observed in food and food products (14.1%); and petty trade (7.8%) than any other business activity.

Table 4.2. Number of operators and owners in different lines of business

Line of Business	Number of operators and owners	Percent	Cumulative percent
Food and food products	26	13.0	13.0
Metal and wood work	37	18.5	31.5
Textile and clothing	21	10.5	42.0
Construction	40	20.0	62.0
Urban agriculture	20	10.0	72.0
Solid waste	5	2.5	74.5
Trade	51	25.5	100.0
Total	**200**	**100.0**	

SOURCE: Field data.

Table 4.3. Gender breakdown of respondents, by business type

Gender	1	2	3	4	5	6	7
Male	3.1%	17.3%	7.8%	18.1%	3.2%	1.8%	9.4%
Female	14.1%	3.8%	3.2%	4.0%	4.0%	2.5%	7.8%

SOURCE: Field data.

Key: 1= Food and food products   4= Construction   7= Petty Trade
      2= Metal and woodwork   5= Urban agriculture
      3= Textile and clothing   6= Municipal services

Men are significantly represented in the construction (18.1%) and metal and wood works (17.3%) business activities. The least representation of both women and men is observed to be in municipal services activity with 2.5% and 1.8%, respectively.

4.1.2. Business location and premises

Business location and premises are critical for business survival. A suitable business location is a key ingredient in business success. Each city and town has prime areas for business depending on the type of business. Table 4.4 shows that 19.5% are located in commercial districts and 26% are located along road sides. These areas seem to be easily accessible sites particularly for customers. A significant portion (19%) undertakes operation in industrial sites. This is positive in that industrial sites are areas designated for production. It is, however, equally important to note that home (18%) and traditional market (6%) are also places from where some businesses operate. These areas are definitely not appropriate for modern businesses that require different facilities and access. It is, therefore, important to make sure that these businesses get appropriate location. A small proportion (7%) of the businesses is mobile businesses. Though their number is small they still need attention since mobile operation compromises with long-term growth of businesses.

Table 4.4. Business location

Business location	Frequency	Percentage
Home	36	18.0
Traditional market	11	5.5
Commercial district	39	19.5
Road side	51	25.5
Mobile	14	7.0
Industrial site	38	19.0
Central road	7	3.5
No response	4	2.0
Total	**200**	**100**

SOURCE: Field data.

In terms of business premise, those who operate under temporary structure (34.5%), in structures that have only roof (6.5%) and no structure (9.5%) in total form 51%, slightly higher than those who operate under permanent structures (47.5%) (Table 4.5). A significant number of operators thus need appropriate premises for their businesses.

Table 4.5. Type of business premises

Business premise	Frequency	Percentage
Permanent structure	95	47.5
Temporary structure	69	34.5
Roof only	13	6.5
No structure	19	9.5
Other	1	0.5
No response	3	1.5
Total	**200**	**100**

SOURCE: Field data.

4.1.3. License and regulation

MSEs are formal businesses and operate legally. The study found out that 86% of the businesses work under license and it is only 14% who have no license. These businesses must be the existing old businesses. Operation under license and legal provision are necessary for businesses since access to various services is dependent on their legal status. Legal status is, therefore, beneficial for the future growth of businesses. The majority indicated that their licenses are issued by the Bureau of Trade and Industry (61%) and Regional government (11.5%). Business owners were asked for their opinion regarding payment for business licenses. It is only 10.5% who complained that payments are high. The remaining did not complain about payments for licenses. This is a positive sign since high payments could discourage businesses from becoming legal and formal.

Licensed and formal businesses operate under law and regulations. Different regulations, such as income tax rate, business law, interest rate, licensing rules, etc., affect the operation of businesses. In fact, one of the reasons for informality in businesses is to escape from hostile rules and regulations. Business owners indicated that laws and regulations are not at all problems for their operations. In fact, 88% indicated that it is not a problem and only 6.5% mentioned that it is fairly problematic.

4.2. Business Operators' Characteristics: Demographic and Socio-Economic Conditions

About 557 business owners and operators were interviewed for the purposes of observing the impact of MSE operations on their livelihood and employment. These operators have shown certain demographic and socio-economic characteristics.

It is interesting to note that the average age of all operators is 31 years of age. This is a clear indication that the youth are the main beneficiaries from the MSE sector. Those operators with age group between 16-30 years form 61.9%, thus indicating that the majority are below the age of 30 (Table 4.6). The gender distribution shows male dominance among operators; and this finding conforms to an earlier observation cited in this study.

Table 4.6. Age and gender distribution of business operators

Age distribution	Frequency	Percentage
16-20	42	7.5
21-30	303	54.4
31-40	149	26.8
41-50	44	7.9
51-60	13	2.3
>60	6	1.07
Gender distribution		
Male	338	60.3
Female	219	39.1

SOURCE: Field data.

Table 4.7 shows that most operators have mid-level educational attainment. Those with secondary education (7-12 Grade) form 58.5% of the respondents. This level of educational attainment is necessary to run micro-businesses which require some level of literacy as businesses involve planning and accounting besides technical knowledge. Those below secondary level of education form 27% and they need to exert extra effort to improve their literacy level in order to properly run their businesses.

Table 4.7. Educational status of operators

Educational level	Frequency	Percentage
None	59	10.6
Primary (1-6)	94	16.9
Junior secondary (7-8)	113	20.3
Senior secondary (9-12)	213	38.2
Diploma	63	11.3
Degree	11	2.0
other	2	0.4
No answer	2	0.4
Total	**557**	**100**

SOURCE: Field data.

Despite attainment of mid-level education by the majority of operators and owners, technical skill is not as widespread. About 55% of the operators have no technical education whatsoever. It is only 18% who reported to have attended technical training institutes and another 1.5% who had polytechnic training. About 2.5% had apprentice training in different technical skills. Therefore, in total, it is only 22% who reported some level and type of technical training. Most micro-enterprises require technical skills. Wood and metal work, construction, textile and clothing assume some technical knowledge and it will be difficult to engage in these businesses without proper mastery of the technical skill. Technical skill training, therefore, seems to be one area in which the MSE offices need to put more work at different levels.

It is also revealing to see that a little less than half of the operators do not have any business training (Table 4.8). This amplifies the training need of the operators. Those who have received business training have only a short duration of training. For example, those with one week of training form 20.3% and those with 1-4 weeks of training form 19.6% (Table 4.8). In total, 40% have reported less than one month of training. It is very difficult to assume that operators can master the training and change behaviors within such a short period of time. The occupational engagement of the interviewed operators in the micro-businesses indicates that most are involved in craft work (36%) and administration (33%). A significant proportion (21.4%) is also working as daily laborers.

Table 4.8. Number and proportion of operators receiving business training

Business training	Frequency	Percentage
None	253	45.4
One week	113	20.3
1-4 weeks	109	19.6
1-3 months	29	5.2
4-12 months	8	1.4
More than a year	6	1.1
No response	39	7.0
Total	**557**	**100**

SOURCE: Field data.

5. Business Development, Growth and Linkages

5.1. Capital and Business Income

The level and growth of capital and business income could be good indicators of the economic performance of firms. Firms with higher and increasing levels of capital signify that capital accumulation is taking place while those with lower trends in capital could be declining enterprises. The following section looks at the initial and current capital to see if capital is growing among MSEs.

5.1.1. Capital

The average initial investment of MSEs in all Regions is approximately 24,000 Birr with those enterprises in Bahir Dar (13,031 Birr) and Adama (13,385 Birr) having a much lower average initial investment (Table 5.1). Enterprises in Hawassa have a much higher average initial investment (45,208 Birr). Initial investment is lower for regular businesses compared to those under the package types. The latter have better access for credit and loan.

The current estimated total capital which includes fixed capital is much higher than the initial investment. For example, the average total capital is 143,000 Birr, which is six times more than the average initial investment. It is interesting to note that the regular and package businesses show no differences in terms of their current total capital. This is an indication of the fact that the regular businesses have a higher capitalization performance than the package programs. In fact, the current total capital of the regular businesses is nearly 10 times more than their initial investment. The package programs have shown only an increase of four fold.

Table 5.1. Average initial, current and working capital, by business types

Business types	Initial capital	Current capital	Working capital
Package businesses	32401.90	142606.55	33324.24
Regular businesses	10184.35	143591.56	16926.32
Total	**23761.74**	**142993.52**	**26587.79**
Towns			
Bahir Dar	13031.10	93186.60	8921.29
Adama	13385.51	98307.00	36545.11
Mekelle	23643.60	231881.00	37846.98
Total	**23761.74**	**142993.52**	**26587.79**

SOURCE: Field data.

In term of business sector, trade, textile and municipal services have low initial capital (Fig 5.1). Perhaps, these businesses do not require high amount of initial capital. Food and food products, urban agriculture and construction have the highest initial capital. These sectors are also the ones which have high current capital as well. In terms of capitalization, however, it is only construction which has registered the highest amount of increment among those which have high initial investment. Its current total capital is almost 8 times higher than its initial investment. Other sectors along this line are trade which has shown an increment of 8.5 times and metal and wood work which has shown an increment of 7.6 times. The fact that trade, though it has low total capital, is one of the sectors with high capital increment needs to be seen in light of the attention it is given. Trade is not considered as a growth sector by the MSE Strategy and hence does not qualify for full package of services as the others. Its level of growth, however, is an indication that it should also be given a greater attention than its present status. Most of the trade activities fall under the regular program.

Fig 5.1. Average initial, working and current capitals by business sectors

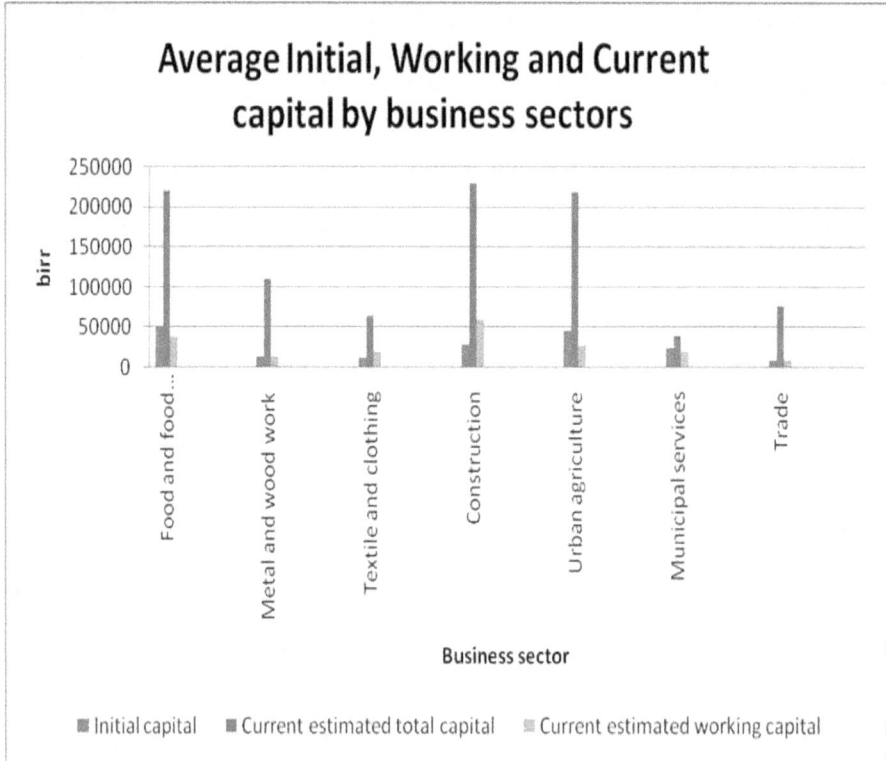

The distribution of capital provides a better picture regarding the nature of capitalization. It can be seen that slightly over half or 54% of the enterprises have an initial capital of less than 5000 Birr (Table 5.2). This is an indication that MSEs have low entry requirement and they start with low amounts of capital. According to the MSE definition of the Ethiopian government, firms with a capital of up to 20,000 Birr are designated as micros. Nearly 70% of the MSEs had initial investment of less than 15,000, which is an indication that the majority were micros at the start up period. A few firms have relatively large capital. For example, those enterprises with an initial capital of more than 50,000

Birr form 14%. These enterprises are more in Hawassa where they form about 23% of the enterprises.

For a significant number of the enterprises (43.6%) the current working capital is less than 5000 Birr with those above 50,000 Birr forming 14% of the total. The working capital thus replicates the patterns seen in the initial investment. The fact that a significant proportion has low working capital means the business operation of the MSEs is limited in nature.

The proportion of MSEs with a total capital of less than 5000 Birr are only 8% while those with a total capital of over 50,000 Birr form 56%. This signifies that the majority of the enterprises have registered a significant increase in their capital amount or capital accumulation process is taking place in most of the firms. This is also an indication that these firms are transferring from micro- to small enterprises. While this is a welcome achievement, the average which is 143,000 Birr is still much lower than the limits for micro- and small enterprises which is a capital of 500,000 Birr. This means the enterprises will stay micro- and small for some time. In other words, the enterprises have to do a lot more in order to transform themselves to medium scale enterprises.

Table 5.2. Proportion of MSEs by initial, total and working capital

Range (Birr)	Initial capital	Current total capital	Working capital
0-3000	37.6	5.1	29.2
3001-5000	16.8	3.1	14.6
5001-10,000	11.7	5.6	16.8
10001-15000	4.1	2.6	7.0
15001-25000	6.6	9.2	10.8
25001-50,000	9.6	18.9	7.6
>50,000	13.7	55.6	14.1

SOURCE: Field data.

5.1.2. Business Income

The gross sales or gross revenue is used to assess the business income of the enterprises. The average weekly sale for all enterprises is 6000 Birr with sales reaching as high as 10,000 Birr in Adama (Table 5.3). Though net revenue will be less than the gross revenue, the figures indicate that the sampled MSEs have higher levels of revenue in comparison with other similar studies in Ethiopia.

For example, Tegegne and Mulat (2004) reported average weekly sales of 524 Birr for micro-enterprises in the small towns of the Amhara Region.

Weekly sales are lower for business in the regular program compared to those in the package programs. This is surprising given the fact that those in the regular businesses have shown higher levels of increase in their capital amount.

Table 5.3. Average weekly sales of enterprises, by town and business type

Town and business type	Weekly total revenue (Birr)
Bahir Dar	1848.47
Adama	10073.79
Hawassa	6121.10
Mekelle	6902.31
Total	**5992.17**
Business type	
Package	7887.06
Regular	3339.33
Total	**5992.17**

Source: Field data.

Weekly sales by sectors show that food and food products and the construction sectors are the ones with higher levels of weekly sales. This is consistent with the above finding that these two sectors have also shown high levels of total capital. Municipal services with only 567 Birr of weekly sale and trade with 1367 Birr of weekly sale have the lowest average revenue.

The distribution of sales by sector shows that about 50% of the MSEs, however, have weekly sales of less than 1000 Birr (Fig 5.3). The proportion of MSEs with weekly sales of up to 2000 Birr reaches nearly two-third (64.3 %). This is an indication that though MSEs have high average sales, the majority of them have low weekly sales or low income.

Sectoral differences are apparent in terms of business income (Table 5.4). The entire MSEs in municipal services reported weekly sales of less than 1000 Birr. An overwhelming majority of enterprises (nearly 80%) in the urban agriculture and textile sectors also have weekly sales of less than 2000 Birr. Enterprises in the construction sector are by far those with a higher level of weekly income. For instance, 47.6% of the enterprises in this sector have a weekly income of more than 5000 Birr while 22% have a weekly income of more than 15,000 Birr. The construction sector must have high demand and high profit. This could be due to the fact the construction sector is highly linked to government projects, such as condominium construction, road building, etc.

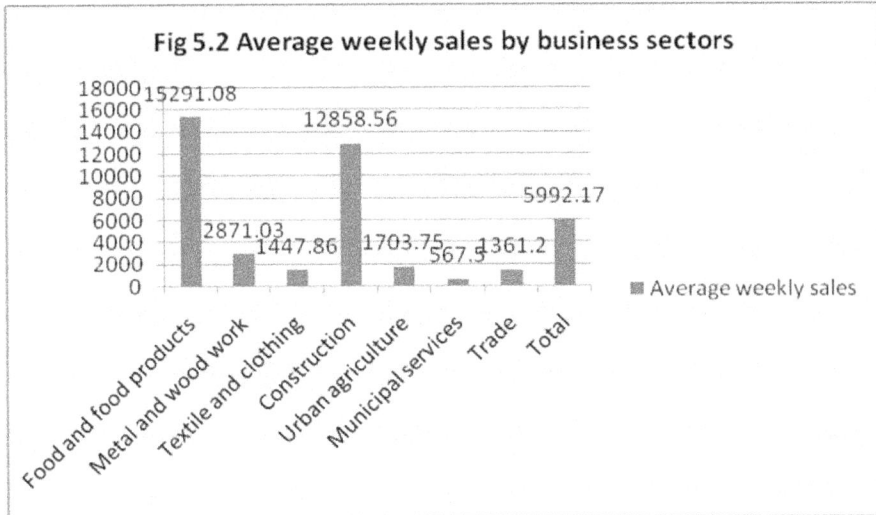

Fig 5.2 Average weekly sales by business sectors

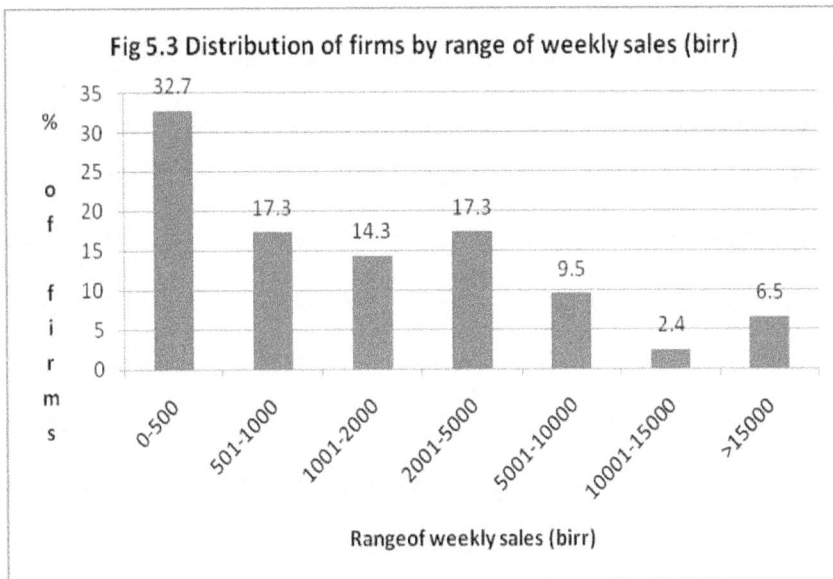

Fig 5.3 Distribution of firms by range of weekly sales (birr)

Table 5.4. Distribution of firms by sectors and weekly sales

Range of weekly sales	Foods and food products	Metal and wood work	Textile and clothing	Construction	Urban agriculture	Municipal services	Trade	Total
0-500	30.8	37.9	47.6	6.3	25.0	50.0	45.0	32.7
501-1000	19.2	13.8	14.3	6.3	31.3	50.0	20.0	17.3
1001-2000	15. 4	10.3	19.0	6.3	25.0	0.0	17.5	14.3
2001-5000	11.5	20.7	14.3	34. 4	12.5	0.0	10.0	17.3
5001-10000	3.8	13.8	4.8	18.8	6.3	0.0	7.5	9.5
10001-15000	3.8	3. 4	0.0	6.3	0.0	0.0	0.0	2. 4
>15000	15. 4	0.0	0.0	21.9	0.0	0.0	0.0	6.5

SOURCE: Field data.

Trend in income is an indication of future growth possibility for enterprises. MSE operators were asked to indicate trends in their income over the last three years. A significant majority or slightly over two-third (64%) indicated that income is increasing. Those enterprises who mentioned that their income is increasing ranged between 57% and 78% across towns. The same picture is painted across sectors as well. This is very encouraging for MSEs since even if most have low income, the prospect of increasing income will give them a reason to stay in the sector and expand the same.

5.2. Business Environment and Competition

5.2.1 Business environment

The business environment for MSEs is fairly favorable. For example, cooperative MSEs are exempted from tax so long as members do not receive dividends. In some Regions, such as the Southern Region, MSEs are given a two-year grace period under the designation of micros that lifts the requirements of tax payment. The MSE operators indicated that policy and regulations such as licensing, registration, tax administration, labor laws, trade regulation are not threats to their operation (Table 5.5). In short, they are not perceived as obstacles. This is significant since norms, customs, policies can either facilitate or hinder the movement of a product or service through the market system (USAID 2008).

The most significant obstacles are access to land, place of operation, lack of market, access to finance and electricity, in that order. These are ranked from first to fifth in terms of severity out of 18 problem items. Access to land and place of operation are related to securing a permanent business premise. This is in fact a major constraining factor both for new starters and for existing MSEs for expansion purposes. Lack of a permanent business premise destabilizes businesses and reduces their sustainability. It has been indicated above that since the provision of land for businesses is not sustainable, there is a change of strategy toward making premises available on rent basis. The demand for these units, however, is extraordinary high and the supply cannot keep pace with the demand.

Despite the fact that efforts are made to create market for the MSEs, 49% believe market availability is the major constraint. As indicated above, MSEs mainly cater to local markets and most benefit from government projects. MSEs, however, need to vigorously pursue market and explore not only local markets but also the national market. Access to the national market can be attained if MSEs are successful in bidding and managing contracts on their own.

Finance is a critical input for MSEs. Finance is also part of the market support service . Micro-finance institutions are the main sources of finance for this sector. It is indicated above that Regional governments provide revolving fund to finance micro-finance institutions. Micro-finance institutions, however, have to balance the needs of micro-enterprises and their operation as business enterprises. In Ethiopia, there is limited involvement of the private sector in micro-enterprise financing. As has been indicated elsewhere in this report, the only exception from the study sites is Adama where some private MFIs like Meklit are also providing loans for micro-enterprises. These enterprises, however, negotiate on their own and they have to pay the market interest rate.

Table 5.5. Problems identified as obstacles by MSEs (% firms)

Item	Moderate obstacle	Major obstacle	Total	Rank
Telecommunication	3.5	11.5	15.0	10
Electricity	11.5	26.5	38.0	5
Transportation	10.5	13.0	23.5	8
Access to land	16.5	43.5	60.0	1

Table 5.5. *Cont'd*

Item	Moderate obstacle	Major obstacle	Total	Rank
Place of operation	19.0	37.5	56.5	2
Lack of market	19.0	29.5	48.5	3
Skill and education of workers	17.0	13.5	30.5	6
Tax rate	5.5	9.5	15.0	10
Tax administration	4.5	8.5	13.0	14
Custom and trade regulation	7.5	6.0	13.5	13
Labor regulation	3.5	1.5	5.0	17
Licensing and registration	1.0	3.0	4.0	18
Access to finance	15.5	30.5	46.0	4
Cost of finance	11.5	13.0	24.5	7
Corruption	4.5	6.5	11.0	15
Crime, theft and disorder	3.5	6.0	9.5	16
Anti competitive practice	7.5	7.0	14.5	12
Economic policy	11.0	12.0	23.0	9

SOURCE: Field data.

5.2.2. Competition

There are two views on competition. On one hand, competition is supposed to enhance productivity and open a way for expansion. Firms which are not competitive cannot sustain themselves particularly if the support they are given is reduced or withdrawn. On the other hand, severe competition can stifle small enterprises which are not capable of competing in the market both in price and non-price parameters.

The MSE operators believe that there are many competitors in the catchment area for their products/services. On average, over 40 competitors are reported to be present in their catchment. The main competitors are formal domestic business (51%). These firms produce the same type of products and services the MSEs provide in the market. This is attested by 78% of the MSEs. The second source of competition comes from the informal sector (26%). Imports are seen less as a threat for the MSEs (2.5%).

Apart from the competition in the catchment area, MSE operators and members also believe that their competitors have better access to raw materials (15.5%), better location (18.5%) and better access to credit (13.0%). These are the dimensions of non-price competition that can easily be overcome by providing access to the MSEs. The fact that location (premise) and finance are given as the competitive advantages of competitors signify the critical nature of these inputs for MSEs success.

It is interesting to note that despite the presence of competitors, particularly from the domestic sources for their products and services, a significant proportion of the MSEs believe that there is market for their products and services (51.5%). On the other hand, about 46.5% believe that their market is constrained by the presence of competitors.

5.3. Business Linkages

5.3.1. Horizontal and vertical linkages (partnership and cooperation)

Inter-firm linkage is key to upgrading. It facilitates collective efficiency, joint ventures, transfer of innovation and opportunities for growth and development. In addition, inter-firm interactions are key to learning, upgrading and fulfilling the domestic market requirements. The particular feature of small enterprises is that they operate in isolation, which decreases their competitiveness.

There are two kinds of cooperation and partnership that firms can engage in. The first is horizontal cooperation and the second is vertical cooperation. Horizontal cooperation allows firms to sub-contract activities, involve in joint action such as joint purchase of inputs, joint marketing, joint labor training, etc. The vertical relationship involves both backward and forward linkages. The supplier-producer relations or input-output relations and the subcontracting of phases of production cycles form vertical linkages.

According to research findings, the majority of MSEs (60%) reported that they do not cooperate with other producers in the same line of business. This is a major deficiency on the part of these firms and is a strong indication that the majority of firms do not have horizontal cooperation with other firms. A significant proportion (35%) of these firms believed that absence of mechanism for cooperation is the major reason for not seeking cooperation with other firms. Other firms believed that there is no trust (10%) and no need for cooperation (13%). Trust is a significant factor for inter-firm cooperation. Its absence is an indication that social capital needs to be strengthened. Generally, economic relations are believed to be embedded in social relations. Such networks could be based on similarity of Regional background, tribe or profession and use trust as their basis. Yu (2000) indicated that small firms can use personal networks when entering into sub-contracting relations to acquire orders or meet seasonal demands and deliver goods in a very short period of time.

Some firms (40%), however, have indicated that they are linked with other firms (table 5.6). Among these, almost all indicated that they are engaged in cooperation with similar firms. Firms were asked about the factors that engendered cooperation among firms. Lack of economies of scale (13%), lack of capacity (10%) and lack of finance (9%) are the major reasons cited as reasons for cooperation. This is an indication that what drives cooperation among small enterprises is the gap between market requirement and producer capability.

It is, however, interesting to note that cooperation is not done on a regular basis. Table 5.6 shows that firms reported that they cooperate only sometimes. Joint labor training, information exchange, sharing and borrowing of machineries and other forms of cooperation are mentioned as being effectuated only sometimes. This shows the lack of regularity. Irregular cooperation is not sustainable and permanent. The little and the infrequent cooperation, mentioned, however, shows that there are no vertical linkages among firms. It is only 7% who mentioned cooperation with bigger firms and another 6% who mentioned cooperation with smaller firms. Vertical linkages are needed because lead firms at the top of the chain have the closest contact with end market and they are the ones which understand the demand condition and market. Therefore, well developed vertical linkages increase price competitiveness as they reduce transaction cost. They are also important for facilitating information transfer, innovation and collective action within a market system (USAID 2008). Vertical linkages have implication for competitiveness and profitability of the micro enterprises and the big firms.

Table 5.6. Proportion of enterprises reporting different forms of cooperation

Forms of cooperation	All the time	Often	Regularly	Sometimes
Exchange of information and experience	5.5	9.5	3.0	14.5
Sharing, borrowing machinery	2.5	4.5	2.0	11.0
Joint marketing of products	2.0	1.5	2.0	9.0

Table 5.6. *Cont'd*

Forms of cooperation	All the time	Often	Regularly	Sometimes
Joint purchase of inputs	1.5	3.5	1.5	8.0
Subcontracting	0.0	2.5	1.0	6.5
Joint labor training	2.5	1.0	6.5	31.0
Undertaking jobs or contracts together	1.0	1.0	2.5	9.0
Sharing the cost of utilities	2.0	2.0	1.5	4.5
Supplying inputs	3.0	3.0	1.0	9.0

SOURCE: Field data.

5.3.2. Local and external linkages

The local and external linkages of business could be examined in terms of input sources and market places for outputs. The input sources and markets were designated as local, Regional and national.

According to field findings, nearly 80.6% of the respondents reported that they procured inputs either from local sources or the Regional capital while only an insignificant 0.5% said they relied on international input sources (Table 5.7). About 8.5% of those surveyed procured inputs from the national capital. This finding conforms with the theoretical postulate spelt out in the literature review section of this study that one of the advantages of MSEs is that they utilize easily available and accessible inputs, preferably from local sources, for the production of goods and services. Hence, the fact that local and Regional sources also constitute main suppliers of inputs for a preponderant number of owners and operators would mean better opportunities and prospects for the growth of MSEs.

Table 5.7. Source of inputs for MSEs in the study area

Source	Number of owners and operators	Percent	Cumulative percent
Local	110	55.0	57.6
Regional capital	44	22.0	80.6
National capital	17	8.5	89.5
Local and Regional capital	6	3.0	92.7
Other towns	1	0.5	93.2
Local and national capital	5	2.5	95.8
Local, Regional and National capital	5	2.5	98.4
International	1	0.5	99.0
Regional and National capital	2	1.0	100.0
Total	**191**	**95.5**	--
No response	9	4.5	--
Total	**200**	**100.0**	**100.0**

SOURCE: Field data.

As with inputs, adequate and reliable markets are key to the success and continued growth of MSEs. In other words, it is generally argued that there should be reliable markets for MSE products and services if these businesses are to be sustainable and profitable ventures. In addition, it is also true that markets must be close to production and service centers. This has the added advantage of reduced transport cost and thus making the enterprises competitive.

This study has found that most enterprises sold their products and services to customers within close proximity to production and service centers. As per the field data, a very high proportion of owners and operators (91.2%) reported that they sold their products and services within the same sub-location, within 5 miles or the Regional capital[4]. This indicates that MSEs cater to local demand and customers and they depend by and large on local income and demand. On

---

[4] Note that the study towns are also regional capitals.

the other hand, the national market is insignificant for the MSEs and therefore exports cannot be used as sources of growth.

5.3.3. Linkage with the local farm sector

There are three ways by which business enterprises could be linked to the farm sector. First, the farm sector is a major provider of inputs. Second, the farm sector is the major market of the small businesses.

Table 5.8 shows that 24.5% or only about one-fourth of the operators use farm produce as their inputs. These inputs, however, come both from local and non-local sources. Those operators who use inputs from local farms form 22%. This is an indication that local backward linkage of businesses to agriculture is limited. In fact, industrial products are the most important inputs for the MSEs. About 39% or well over one-third of the operators reported using industrial products.

Table 5.8. Types of inputs used, by businesses

Types of inputs	Frequency	Percentage
Local farm produce	44	22
Non-local farm produce	2	1.0
Local and non-local farm produce	3	1.5
Industrial products	78	39.0
Locally available raw materials	32	16.0
Local raw materials and industrial products	13	6.5
Others	19	9.5
No response	9	4.5
Total	**200**	**100**

SOURCE: Field data.

In terms of market linkage, local agriculture has even a more limited role. It is indicated in Table 5.9 that town dwellers and institutions are by far the most important customers for the MSEs. Nearly 90% of the MSEs rely on town dwellers and institutions as their market sources.

The fact that the MSE sector has limited backward linkage with the farm sector and practically no market linkage does not tie up well with the objective of the MSE strategy which in fact attempts to foster rural-urban linkages. This should stand out as an important finding because it is indicative of the very limited rural-urban economic linkage, and thus can be a brake on the further growth of the MSE sector. It also points to the need for reorienting the MSE strategy towards a direction that will create effective linkages between the urban and rural economies.

Table 5.9. Type of customers of MSEs

Type of customer	Frequency	Percentage
Town dwellers	118	59.0
Farmers	2	1.0
Town dwellers and farmers	5	2.5
Institutions	37	18.5
Town dwellers and institutions	24	12.0
Town dwellers, institutions and farmers	5	2.5
Others	7	3.5
No response	2	1.0
Total	**200**	**100**

SOURCE: Field data.

5.4. Service Needs and Assistance Received

MSEs owners and operators were asked to identify critical service areas that they need to make their businesses profitable and worthwhile. This was an important issue to make the assistance relevant and demand-responsive to the needs and priorities of the businesses. This consideration was also essential to prioritize areas of intervention given the capacity and resource constraints faced by Regional and city government MSE bureaus/sector offices.

According to research findings, respondents categorized their needs into 3 critical service areas in order of importance. In the first critical service category, micro-finance (37.7%), production and marketing space (30.2%), market linkage (6.5%), and training (4.0%) were rated as main areas of concern. In the second category, micro-finance (28.0%); production and marketing space (20.6%), market linkage (12.7%), and training (11.1%) were identified as the next important list of priorities. Training (23.3%), marketing and production space (16.5%), micro-finance (12.8%), and market linkage (12.0%) were categorized as third-level issues of concern. What emerges from this finding is that a similar set of concerns, viz. micro-finance, training, market linkage, marketing and production space in a convenient location, were identified as very much needed service areas by an average of 72.8% of the respondents. This finding is useful to determine areas of intervention to help the growth of the MSE industry, and insure effective coordination of the activities of the different stakeholders engaged in assisting the sector.

In line with the MSE development strategy, Regional and city governments have set up bureaus and sector offices. These provide various kinds of assistance to operators and members of newly established and already operating businesses. Such assistance is vital in ensuring the sustainability and growth of the businesses. When asked about the details, respondents confirmed that they had received various kinds of assistance, including financial training (18.5%), getting production and marketing space (14.5%), and finance, production and marketing space assistance (15.9%). Assistance received in technical training (4.5%) and management training (1.5%) constituted the third important category of service needs. An important point to note here is that the proportion of MSEs who received assistance is small. This is an indication of the fact that service coverage is limited and there is a need for far more scaling up and outreaching the majority of the businesses.

A related concern in service delivery other than its coverage is adequacy, relevance and timeliness of services. The promotional strategy must be based on the needs and priorities of business owners and operators to have any meaningful impact on the inter-related goals of employment creation, income generation and poverty reduction. Based on a sample of responses, the majority of business owners and operators did not positively rate some of the services they received. While the causes for the negative reaction can be varied, all point to the need for improvements in approach and strategy of assistance provision. In addition, the feedback should also serve as a reminder to carry out a thorough feasibility assessment of the needs and challenges of the businesses so that the assistance is demand-driven, instead of being supply-side dictated, as seems to be the case currently. Figure 5.4 depicts the level of dissatisfaction with selected kinds of assistance.

Figure 5.4. Assessment of selected services by MSE owners and operators

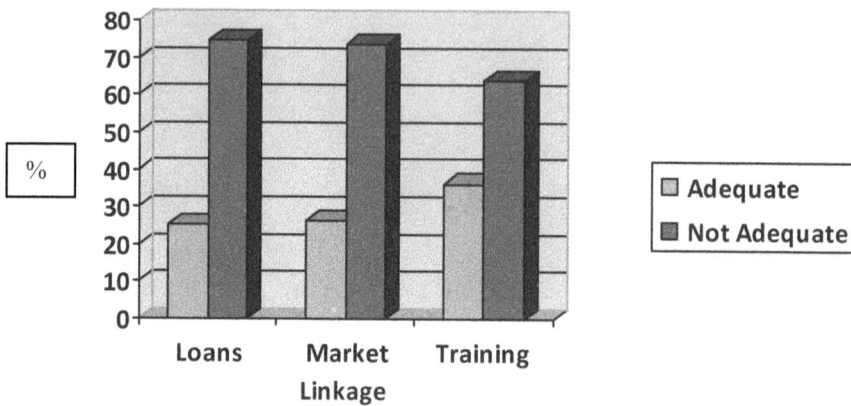

SOURCE: Field data.

As can be observed from Figure 5.4, most operators and owners were dissatisfied with the services offered to them by MSE development bureaus and sector offices. For example, when it comes to the provision of loans, only 25.3% of the respondents were happy with the credit that they received while the overwhelming majority (74.7%) reported a great deal of dissatisfaction. Possible explanations for such discontent may relate to the inadequate amounts and strict terms of the loans, including stringent collateral requirements and short repayment periods

When it comes to market linkage too, the situation is not much different— only 26.3% of the respondents reported some degree of satisfaction while 73.7% were grossly unhappy with the quality of service provided. By the same token, only 36.2% of the respondents who were offered training services were happy with the quality of the service provided while a significant 63.8% were not happy at all. In both cases, the survey results suggest a reassessment of the current training provided to MSEs and an enhanced effort to create effective inter-sectoral and rural-urban market linkages in the marketing of goods and services as well as supply of inputs.

5.5. Graduation and Future Plan

MSEs are expected to graduate once they reach the capital limit of ETB 500,000. It was earlier indicated that the present level of capital (ETB 143,000) of MSEs is significantly lower than the requirements. MSEs were asked regarding their perception on the issue. About 59% of the micros are optimistic that they will graduate from the micro someday while 40% are pessimistic in that they do not think they are capable of graduating. While the presence of optimistic enterprises indicates the promises of the MSE strategy, the presence of pessimistic enterprises casts doubt on the possibility of the micros being able to transform themselves.

It is quite interesting to note that there is Regional variation in MSEs' perception on graduation. The overwhelming majority of those in Tigray (87.5%) are optimistic as opposed to only 35% in Hawassa (Table 5.10). Such Regional differences signal that there are differences in the prospects and constraints MSEs face in different Regions.

Table 5.10. Firms' perception on graduation

Will you graduate from micro- and small scale enterprises?	Bahir Dar	Adama	Hawassa	Mekelle	Total
Yes	54.0	62	34.6	87.5	59.3
	(27)	(31)	(17)	(42)	(117)
No	46	38	65.3	12.5	40.6
	(23)	(19)	(32)	(6)	(80)

SOURCE: Field data.

Out of the 40% of the total MSEs or 80 enterprises which were pessimistic about graduation, 61 enterprises indicated four major reasons for their pessimism. These are 'businesses are not growing (33), 'lack of finance' (13), 'lack of market' (11) and lack of working place (4).

These reasons vary by Region (Table 5.11). In Hawassa, 20 out of 25 enterprises from these groups indicated that their business is not growing. In Bahir Dar, all the reasons seem to be fairly represented while in Adama finance is considered as a critical factor by more number of firms.

51

Table 5.11 Major reasons for not being able to graduate from micro- and small
scale enterprises (Number of firms)

Reasons	Bahir Dar	Adama	Hawassa	Mekelle	Total
Business is not growing	6	2	20	5	33
Lack of finance	6	6	1	0	13
Lack of market	7	1	3	0	11
Lack of working place	-	-	-	-	4

SOURCE: Field data.

6. Employment and Changes in Livelihood

6.1. Employment and Previous Employment Status

6.1.1. Employment

Aggregate official figures show that the MSEs have generated quite a
substantial number of employment opportunities in different Regions.
Table 6.1 presents data on employment created by MSEs in 2009 for the
whole of Tigray and Mekelle city. The MSEs have been able to generate
employment for 51,665 people for the whole Region while in Mekelle
city alone they created employment for 18,532 people. Of these, 54%
were females both at the Regional and city levels. This is an indication
that females have a high participation rate in MSEs. Construction is by far
the most important sector for employment. The sector is dominated by
males. Services and trade follow. Both at Regional and city levels,
females dominate the services and trade sector.

Table 6.1. Employment created by MSEs in 2009 in Tigray and Mekelle

Job sector	Tigray			Mekelle		
	Male	Female	Total	Male	Female	Total
Construction	20,998	5,925	26923	7598	2107	9705
Metal and wood work	1929	486	2415	395	150	545
Urban agriculture	4301	2754	7055	1018	1527	2545
Textile and clothing	859	727	1586	384	338	722
Service and trade	6578	7752	14330	2646	2369	5015
Others	558	197	755	-	-	
Total	**33666**	**17999**	**51665**	**12041**	**6491**	**18532**

SOURCE: Tigray micro- and small enterprise agency, unpublished.

Similarly, Table 6.2 indicates the growth of MSE employment in the Amhara Region. Between 2005 and 2009, employment in the Region has increased 11 times while in Bahir Dar city employment has grown twice over the period 2006-2009. The fact that female employment in the Amhara Region is about 57% of the total employment repeats the pattern observed in Tigray and conforms with the higher participation rate of females in MSEs.

Table 6.2. Employment in Amhara Region and Bahir Dar town

Year	Amhara Region			Bahir Dar		
	Male	Female	Total	Male	Female	Total
2005	9286	5490	14776	NA	NA	
2006	26010	14561	40571	NA	NA	4581
2007	47039	26042	73081	NA	NA	3587
2008	58461	34227	92688	NA	NA	5760
2009	102394	58626	161020	NA	NA	8870

SOURCE: Amhara Region, Micro-enterprise Agency, unpublished.

Employment in the sampled MSEs indicates that a total of 3,829 people are involved in different Regions (Table 6.3). This represents 19 workers per enterprise. Of the total employees, 2,174 or 56.7% are entrepreneurs or members of the enterprises. These individuals are collective or sole owners of the enterprises. The MSEs have hired about 1,196 paid workers which is 31.2% of the total people engaged in the sampled enterprises. The ratio of hired labor to members is 0.55, i.e., for every member or owner there is on average 0.55 hired employee. Unpaid workers (5.7%) and apprentices (6.2%) also form part of the labor force engaged in the MSEs though these are reported by a few enterprises.

Table 6.3. Total number of workers engaged in sampled MSEs

Workers	Package			Regular			Total
	Male	Female	Total package	Male	Female	Total regular	
Working members	188	761	1949	303	122	425	2174
Paid workers	619	280	899	198	99	297	1196
Unpaid workers	58	122	180	20	19	39	219
Apprentice	161	68	229	2	9	11	240
Total	2026	1231	3257	523	249	772	3829

SOURCE: Field data.

In terms of sex distribution, females represent 39% of the total people engaged in the MSEs. This proportion is lower than the aggregate figures reported above.

A significant difference in levels of employment is seen between the package and regular business. The total members in the package programs are 1949. Of this, 39% or 761 members are females. These members are entrepreneurs or owners of the MSEs. Those MSEs in the regular program have a total membership of 425 with 29% of these being females.

Both the regular and the package businesses hire labor. This has a far reaching implication for employment creation because every enterprise contributes to additional employment beyond owners. A total of 899 paid workers are employed under the package programs and the figure is about 300 employees for the regular businesses. Package programs have a higher capacity of employing hired labor as their mean hired labor is higher than the regular program. The mean hired labor is 9.8 and 8 for males and females, respectively, in the package programs and 4.8 and 3.5 for males and females, respectively, in the regular program (Table 6.4).

Table 6.4. Current average number of workers per enterprise

Workers	Package		Regular	
	Male	Female	Male	Female
Working members	13.98	9.76	6.31	3.39
	(85)	(78)	(48)	(36)
Paid workers	9.83	8.00	4.83	3.54
	(63)	(35)	(41)	(28)
Unpaid workers	6. 44	10.17	2.22	2.11
	(9)	(12)	(9)	(9)
Apprentice	26.83	13.60	1..0	2.25
	(6)	(5)	(2)	(4)

SOURCE: Field data.

Note: Figures in parenthesis are reporting firms.

6.1.2. Previous employment status and reasons for joining the MSE sector

A significant proportion of the MSE operators (49%) were unemployed prior to joining the MSE sector (Table 6.5). Of these 7.2% declared they stayed at home, 2.7% were too young to work. The remaining 51% of the operators were somehow previously employed in one or another form. Of these, 32.5% were employees of other businesses while 14.2% were undertaking similar or different line of businesses on their own.

The two dominant reasons for joining the MSE sector are lack of options (50%) and preference to work for oneself (40%) (Fig 6.1). Those who gave reasons as lack of options must be those unemployed prior to joining the sector while those who preferred to work for themselves must be those who were previously working as employees of either family or non-family business. People do not join the MSE sector because it provides better income. It is only 5% who thought the sector provides better income or they want to diversify their income (4%). Theoretically there are two views of the micro-enterprise sector. The first one considers workers in the micro-enterprise sector as either unemployed or surplus labor. These workers do not find jobs in the formal sector due to their low skills and unemployability. This is the view of the underemployed. The second view focuses on the fact that workers choose this sector for its flexibility and earning opportunity. This is the micro-entrepreneur view (Orlando and Pollack 2000). The first view suggests a high level of poverty in the sector while the second view implies that poverty is not a necessary condition. Our data seem to support the first view. MSE operators in the Ethiopian case enter the sector due to some level of poverty. This is attested to by their response that they had no other options and that they did not choose the micro-sector to gain higher income or diversify their income.

Table 6.5. Employment status before joining MSEs

Employment status	%
Unemployed	38.6
Stayed at home	7.2
Too young to work	2.7
Paid employee in the same line of work	16.2
Paid employee in other line of work	12.2
Operated small business in same line of work	8.6
Operated small business in other line of work	5.6
Farmer	1.6
Self employed	7.0
Total	**99.6**

SOURCE: Field data.

Fig 6.1 Reasons for joining the MSE sector by respondents

To supplement income
4%

No answer
1%

Preference of self employment
40%

No options available
50%

Small businesses provide better income
5%

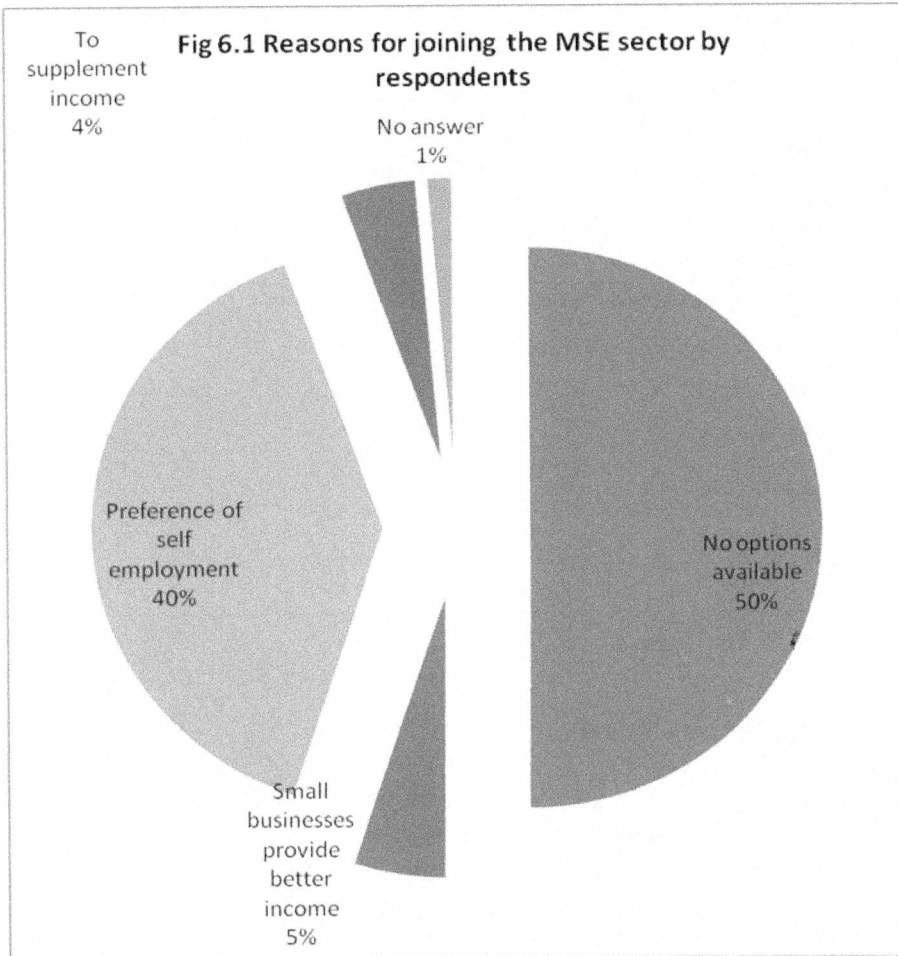

While lack of choices or preference for self-employment may be reasons for joining the MSE sector in general, particular sectors of engagement are chosen on the basis of some reasons (Table 6.6). Skill possession (36.6%) is the major reason for most operators to join a particular sector. This is in line with the criteria of organizing operators by the MSE agencies. As indicated above, one of the criteria in recruiting operators is possession of skills. In this regard, TVET graduates are favored since they possess some skill. The other major reason, which is family engagement in the sector (25%), indicates operators' familiarity with the activity in a particular sector. This facilitates easy adaptation with the requirement of the sector. An equally important reason in sector selection is operators' perception of its profitability (25%). Operators thus choose activities which they think are profitable and provide a higher income. This is a rational decision on the part of operators.

Table 6.6. Reasons for joining a particular MSE sector

Reasons for choosing a particular sector	Percent
Skilled in the activity	36.6
Family has worked in the activity	24.6
Profitability	25.0
Affordability	9.0
No alternative	2.7
No answer	2.2
Total	**100**

SOURCE: Field data.

6.2. Change in Livelihood

The livelihood impact of MSEs could be discerned by looking at the levels and changes in asset, consumption and income. Regarding the latter, since most MSE operators have stayed in the operation for short periods of time, it is quite possible to assume that the influence of factors other than MSEs are negligible in causing changes in asset possession, consumption and income.

6.2.1. Asset levels and change in assets

MSE operators were asked to describe their asset status before and after joining the enterprises either in the forms of cooperatives or private business. Table 6.7 and Figure 6.2 provide the asset levels and changes in asset ownership. First, it can be noted that asset ownership, particularly productive asset ownership, is very poor among operators and members. The only notable asset possession that can be discerned is household durables. It can be seen that those who possess TVs and radios are by far higher than those who possess productive assets. TVs and radios, however, cannot be a significant hedge against shocks since they can easily lose value. Some assets are very critical for the urban poor. For example, housing is the most valuable single possession of the poor in urban areas. In urban areas, housing is equated with land for rural people. A house is an asset that can be used not only to protect oneself from the vagaries of weather but is also an important asset on which income generating activities can be based. For example, home-based enterprises are important for home-bound households (Moser and Holland 2008). Renting houses is also an important source of income (ibid). The poor possession level of houses, both residential and business premises, indicates the low level of assets of the poor. In general, it does not appear that households have significant assets to fall back in time of emergency or shocks.

In terms of changes in asset possession, it is quite possible to see that there are some positive changes. There is a 6% change in residential possession due to MSEs and there is also a 4% increase in vehicle possession. The most significant increase, however, is in the possession of household durables, particularly TV and radio. With a 1% change, possession of a business premise has not changed significantly among operators. While some changes in asset ownership could be discerned, it is quite possible to see that the changes are not very significant.

Table 6.7. Percentage of MSE operators reporting possession of assets

Type of assets	Before joining the MSE	After joining the MSE	Change in percentage of operators
Residential house	9.2	15.1	5.9
Business premise	2.2	3.1	1.1
Vehicle	1.6	5.7	4.1
TV	21.0	37.7	16.7
Radio	37.5	45.8	8.3
Refrigerator	7.5	13.8	6.3

SOURCE: Field data.

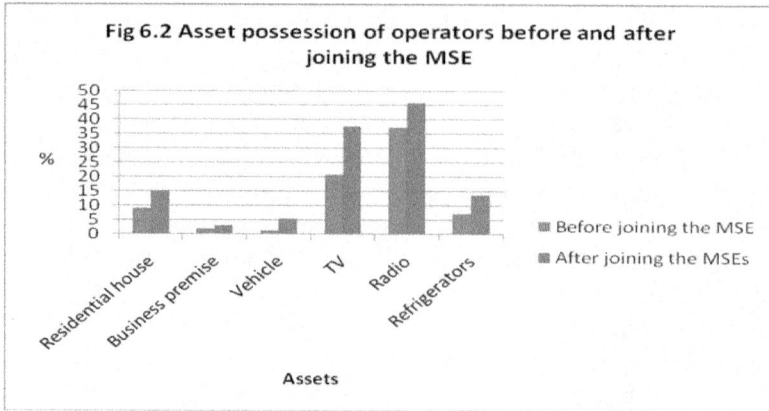

Fig 6.2 Asset possession of operators before and after joining the MSE

SOURCE: Field data.

6.2.2. Income levels and change in income and savings

The average level of monthly income reported by the respondents was 761 Birr with the highest level being for Mekelle with 1180 Birr per month (Table 6.8). In Hawassa, MSE operators get an average of 487 Birr per month. This is the lowest average income among all cities.

Table 6.8. Mean monthly income of entrepreneurs (Birr)

Town	Income
Hawassa	486.75
Mekelle	1179.64
Bahir Dar	737.58
Adama	779.03
Total	**761.41**

SOURCE: Field data.

The proportion of respondents by income range shows that most of the operators have low income. About 27% receive income below 300 (Figure 6.3). Three hundred Birr per month is almost the poverty line in Ethiopia. The proportion of respondents with an income range below 600 Birr reaches 62%. A few individuals receive higher income. For instance, 12% receive monthly incomes above 1,500 Birr.

Fig 6.3 Proportion of respondents by income range

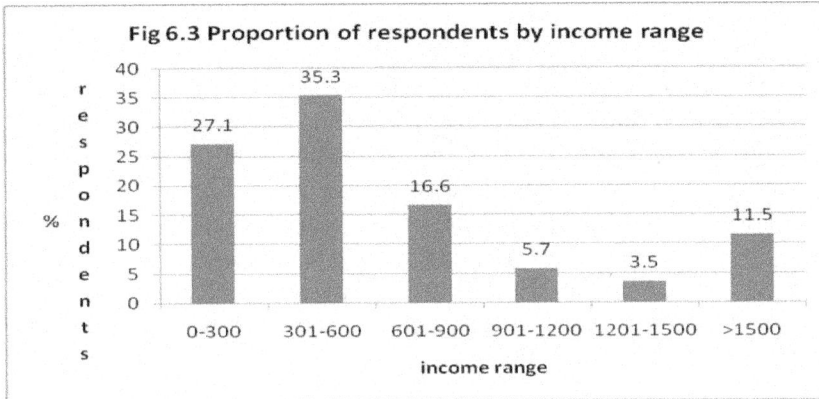

SOURCE: Field data.

Gender differences in monthly income are very noticeable as 45% of the females receive less than 300 Birr. This is a little less than half of those females engaged in MSEs. This is quite different for male workers. Males who receive income less than 300 Birr are only 17%. About three-quarters of the females get income less than 600 Birr while the comparable figure for males is slightly higher than 50%. And 14% of males are in the highest income group earning a monthly income higher than 1500 Birr while only 7% of females are in this group.

Fig 6.4 Proporton of respondents by income range and gender

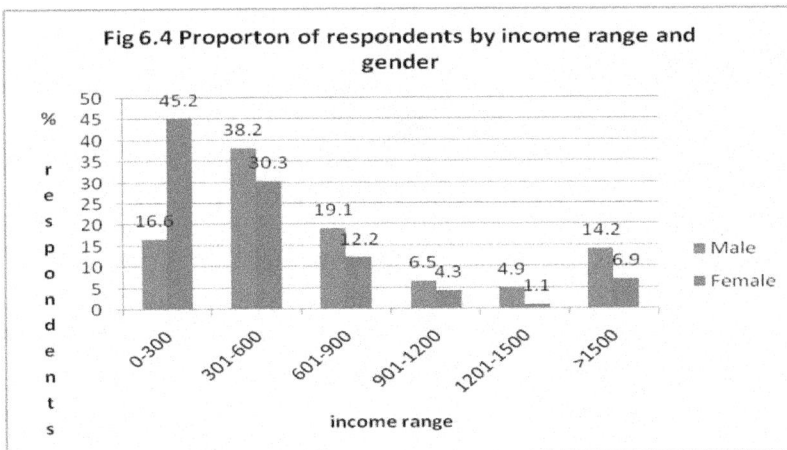

SOURCE: Field data.

It seems that there is some relation between monthly income and education. Those with lower level of education are concentrated in the lower income range. For example, 76% of those who have no education receive income less than 600 Birr (Table 6.9). In contrast, it is only 57% of those with secondary, 51% of those with diploma and 36% of those with degree levels of education who are found in this income range. In other words, as the level of education increases, the proportion of operators in the lowest income group declines. The modal class for all education groups is the 301-600 income range except for those with junior secondary school education. The proportion of those in this modal class, however, shows a declining trend with increased level of education. Moreover, workers with degree level of education depict another modal class, which is the income range between 901-1200.

Table 6.9. Respondents by income range and education level

Income range	None	Primary	Junior Secondary	Secondary	Diploma	Degree
0-300	36.7	28.9	32.4	25.1	16.4	9.1
301-600	38.8	48.2	29.5	32.5	34.4	27.3
601-900	14.3	8.4	15.2	20.2	19.7	18.2
901-1200	0	2.4	6.7	5.9	9.8	27.3
1201-1500	4.1	2.4	4.8	2.5	4.9	9.1
>1500	6.1	9.6	11.4	12.8	14.8	9.1

SOURCE: Field data.

Income from their businesses is the main source of livelihood for the operators. It is only 23% of the operators who reported additional source of income (Table 6.10). It is, therefore, quite safe to assume that MSEs are the major sources of income for the majority of the operators. Out of the non-MSE source of additional income, the major one was found to be wage labor (18 individuals) and assistance from relatives (18 individuals). Farming and remittances are less important as additional sources of income.

Table 6.10. Frequency of operators with additional sources of income

Sources of income	Yes	% of total
	Frequency	
Whether operators have other sources of income	128	23
Sources of income		
Paid government employment	8	1.4
Private/NGO	13	2.3
Wage work	18	3.2
Remittance	6	1.1
Assistance from nearby relatives	18	3.2
Crop farming	5	0.9
Poultry	2	0.4
Other	30	5.4

SOURCE: Field data.

It is interesting to note that operators and owners mainly use their income for household needs. Thus slightly more than half (52.2%) use MSE income for household needs while another 11.1% also use it for paying for their children's education, health and household needs (Table 6.11). In total, therefore, 63.3% or nearly two-third use their MSE income for household maintenance. It is only 19% who use income for business expansion, investment or saving while another 17% mix investment and household maintenance.

As has been indicated above, nearly 63.3% or about two-third of the respondents use income from their MSE operations for household maintenance. This is a positive outcome of the MSE strategy because it has enabled previously unemployed members of society to lead independent livelihoods as productive citizens and income earners. However, the fact that a lion's share of the operators' income is spent on consumption while a relatively less significant portion of the total income is directed towards investment in expanding and strengthening the businesses raises a concern of a different nature. This relates to the long-term sustainability of the businesses. Simply put, unless additional investment is poured back to expand and develop the enterprises, there is less likelihood for these businesses to be viable in the long run and become competitive actors for markets, raw materials and employment generation.

Table 6.11. Use of income from MSEs

Use of income	Frequency	%
Use for household needs	291	52.2
Reinvest in business	91	16.3
Use for children's education and medical expense	43	7.7
Saving	17	3.1
Household need and saving	25	4.5
Household need, children's education, medical expense and saving	19	3.4
Others (invest in agriculture, children's education)	--	12.8

SOURCE: Field data.

The changes in income and savings were recorded for the period before and after joining the MSEs (Table 6.12). In terms of income, it can be seen that there is more than 100% increase in the two study towns and between 84 - 92% increase in the other two study towns. These income changes are significant and clearly depict the extent of improvement in the operators' livelihood. The increase in income, however, has to be seen in light of the rising inflation. It is, therefore, safe to assume that in terms of the real impact the changes may not be significant in raising actual incomes.

The changes in savings for different towns, however, are not evenly distributed across the sample cities. For example, Mekelle (193.97%) and Adama (182.39) have shown quite striking increases in levels of saving (Table 6.12). On the other hand, in the other study towns, viz. Hawassa and Bahir Dar, there is a decline in the level of savings. This is a significant finding because it affects 50% of the sample cities. Many possible explanations can be offered for this state of affairs. One possible pointer may be what is often referred to as the real income effect. That is even though incomes might have increased in nominal terms, real incomes might have gone down due to inflation, thus making it difficult for operators to save from their income. An alternative explanation may be that operators in Bahir Dar and Hawassa might have had higher average levels of expenditures compared to their counterparts in Adama and Mekelle. Further research is needed to establish the exact reasons.

Table 6.12. Average yearly income and savings before and after joining the MSEs

City	Average yearly income (Birr)			Average saving (Birr)		
	Before joining MSEs	After joining MSEs	Percent change	Before joining MSEs	After joining MSEs	Percent change
Hawassa	2988.00	6955.48	132.78	2524.17	2310.53	-8.46
Mekelle	7616.78	14600.42	91.68	3489.47	10258.28	193.97
Bahr Dar	4799.48	8876.45	84.94	2810.36	2745.35	-2.31
Adama	3703.45	13322.69	259.73	2293.75	6477.36	182.39
Total	**4565.90**	**10235.78**	**124.17**	**2839.62**	**5552.21**	**95.52**

SOURCE: Field data.

6.2.3. Change in consumption

Change in consumption could be directly related to improvements in well being. As individuals' income improves the proportion of their income spent on non-food items will increase. Table 6.13 shows the change in expenditure in non-food items particularly on basic services. It can be seen that there is an increase in the average expenditure levels of respondents on education, health, utilities and transport. Such an increase could be directly related to the income of individuals. It could, however, be related to price change, life cycle changes (such as increase in family size), etc. What is interesting in our case is that the number of respondents who consumed a particular item has increased after joining the MSEs. This is an indication that more people are affording to consume these services. The increase in the number of people consuming a particular item is, therefore, a positive impact emanating from MSE operation.

Table 6.13. Average expenditure of respondents before and after joining the MSEs on selected items

Expenditure item	Before joining the MSE (Birr)		After joining the MSE (Birr)	
	Mean expenditure	Number of respondents reporting	Mean expenditure	Number of respondents reporting
Education	127.2	107	252.2	106
Health	112.26	156	122.22	243
Utilities	77.11	216	110.66	449
Transport	68.69	147	99.9	284

SOURCE: Field data.

6.2.4. The perception of MSE operators and owners on their livelihood

In order to corroborate the hard data on livelihood impact, respondents were asked about their perception on their livelihood. Accordingly, 62% of the respondents consider themselves as non-poor or middle-income individuals (Table 6.14). With their monthly income of about 761 Birr, most MSE operators and owners feel they are no more in the poor category. This is a positive outcome because people's perception about their livelihood can indicate their status better. In fact, a significant majority or 78% also believed that they have experienced changes in their livelihood since joining the MSE sector. Concerning the type of changes, most (40%) believe that they are now self-sufficient and able to lead an independent life (Table 6.15). Others (18.5%) believe that they are able to support their family and still others feel (12%) that they are able to generate income. These perceptions more or less agree with the hard data observed above in terms of positive changes in income and consumption levels. Similarly, the majority (56%) would like to stay in the same job while it is only 16% who wanted to change their present jobs (Table 6.16)

Table 6.14. Respondents' perception on their livelihood

How do you rate yourself?	Frequency	%
Poor	202	36.3
Non-poor (middle income)	344	61.8
Rich	10	1.8
Change in livelihood:		
Yes	436	78.3
No	119	21.4

SOURCE: Field data.

Table 6.15. Types of changes perceived by operators

Changes	Frequency	%
Self-sufficient and leading independent life	202	40.2
Able to support family	103	18.5
Able to generate income	66	11.8
Self-sufficient and support family	23	4.1
Self-sufficient, support income and able to income	9	1.6

SOURCE: Field data.

Table 6.16. Future plan of MSE operators

Future plan	Frequency	%
Stay in the same job	312	56.0
Change jobs	89	16.0
Start own MSE	130	23.3
Others	8	1.4

SOURCE: Field data.

7. Successes, Challenges and Policy Issues in the MSE Strategy

7.1. The Successes of the MSE Strategy

The objectives of the MSE development strategy in urban development are the reduction of poverty and unemployment and fostering rural-urban linkages. Poverty is a multidimensional phenomenon. It has both income and non-income dimensions. In tackling poverty, MSEs are supposed to influence these dimensions of poverty. Engagement in the sector has clearly brought income gain for the beneficiaries. Though the income level is low for most beneficiaries and there is also gender disparity in the levels of income, there is undeniable gain in the income of beneficiaries. The clear positive change in the income level of operators and members before and after joining the MSE sector shows that there is an improvement in the income levels of beneficiaries. The fact that these businesses are the primary source of livelihood for the beneficiaries is also an indication of the extent to which MSEs are becoming the fundamental pillar for beneficiaries for their livelihood. This gain in income level has also translated into positive changes in the level of consumption of basic services such as education, health, and transport. These are aspects of non-income dimension of poverty.

The fact that the MSE sector has generated employment not only for the operators but also for hired laborers as well is a clear indication of the importance of the sector in fighting urban unemployment. It is also particularly important to stress the kind of employment created. Most MSE operators are the youth, which is an indication of the importance of the sector for prompting youth employment. According to the recent census, the urban youth within the age group 20-39 form 36% of the total urban population. Those in the age group 15-19 alone form 16.45%. In the study cities, it was found out that 61% of the operators belong to the age group of 16-30, with the overwhelming majority found in the age group of 20-30. It is, therefore, significant that the sector is providing employment for this segment of the population. In addition to the youth employment, the fact that female employment is significant in the sector is itself an added value. Females living in urban areas form 50.3% of the urban population. The study showed that in Tigray Region, 54% of those employed are females while in Amhara Region 57% of those employed are females. In the four study towns, the proportion of females employed were found out to be 39%. The MSE sector thus has a clear benefit for those engaged in this line of economic activity.

It is also quite possible to discern other non-quantifiable impacts that derive from the MSE sector. The fact that a huge number of these businesses are now operating in different towns of the country as a result of the strategy implies that goods and services which are needed and consumed by the local people are now produced. This has a potential of making goods and services available, stabilizing prices and substituting imports. The MSE sector, particularly the construction business, has a potential for supporting other programs such as housing development by producing the various inputs, such as pre-cast beams, hollow blocks, etc. It has also made its contribution to improving the urban environment as MSEs are engaged in the construction of local roads using cobble stones, etc. Similarly, those MSEs engaged in municipal waste collection are also helping improve the urban environment.

7.2. The Challenges of the MSE Strategy

The MSEs program faces numerous challenges that need to be surmounted in order to ensure smooth functioning and sustainability. The challenges come from the nature and adequacy of the support services, the status of the business in terms of expansion and competition, the attitudes of the beneficiaries towards entrepreneurship, etc.

7.2.1. Nature and adequacy of the support services

It was previously highlighted that there are a range of support services provided to the MSE sector in order to ensure sustainability and growth in the economy. These include finance, premise, training, market linkages, etc.

In terms of finance, it has been found out that it is one of the most pressing constraints of the micro-enterprises industry. Financial availability, however, in the form of loan is not enough. There is a serious demand and supply gap. This is manifested in the form of backlogs of financial requests that roll over to other years in different Regions. Indeed, it was found out that many MSEs are registered and licensed but cannot start operations because of lack or shortage of micro-credit. It was realized that this problem has been a serious brake in the start up of new MSE firms by individuals, partnerships and cooperatives in the four cities.

The availability of business premises in adequate quantity and at convenient locations is a serious challenge in the implementation of the MSE development strategy. According to the policy document, there is an intention of allocating 4900 hectares of land for the development of the sector in different cities and towns of the country. The provision of land for expansion has been implemented and the study showed that a sizeable land has already been allotted in different Regions. The competing use of land in urban areas and its scarcity in cities constitute significant constraints for MSE development. As a result, a policy shift towards availing buildings on rent basis is noted. The demand, however, still lags behind the supply and there is a challenge of getting land at the required locations.

The provision of market linkage and training has its own limitations. In terms of training, the nature, relevance and adequacy are not well thought out and coordinated. In many cases, training programs are for a short period of time which may not be adequate to impart skills. The relevance of training for the specific type of job also needs to be evaluated. In this regard, the comment made by key informants in the Amhara Region that training provided by technical colleges are not well integrated into practice is instructive.

MSEs need markets in order to survive and sustain. The effort in different parts of the study cities to provide market linkage, particularly with government institutions, has helped these businesses to gain a continuous demand for their products. Two problems crop up from this arrangement, however. First, not all of the enterprises are beneficiaries of this market linkage policy. It is only those businesses whose products are demanded by government institutions, such as prisons, universities and housing agencies, which are able to gain from such arrangements. Second, though Regional governments try to convince institutions to form market linkages, the latter have options to invite private sector participants as well. Under this circumstance, MSEs which were dependent on government institutions will find it increasingly difficult to sustain themselves.

7.2.2. Business expansion and competition

The prospects for businesses depend on their ability to invest, expand and compete in the local, national and international markets. Our study revealed that MSEs have registered capital growth. The average capital has grown to 143,000 Birr from an initial average capital of 24,000 Birr. This is commendable and needs to be continued. The average attained so far, however, shows that there is a need for further growth in order to graduate from the MSE status and change into medium-level industries. The fact that the prospect for graduation from the MSE sector is bleak is worrisome. Another worrying aspect, however, is operators by and large use their income for household maintenance rather than business expansion.

Similarly, MSEs have indicated that they face a number of competitors, particularly from the formal sector. Both domestic and international competition requires improving one's competitiveness in terms of product quality, prices, delivery time, etc. These aspects of competition do not figure prominently in the operation of MSEs though a significant proportion of these enterprises believes that they have market for their products. Competition also entails being able to compete in the market without subsidy from the government. The MSEs, however, are heavily subsidized with lavish government support, including provision of credit at low rates; free technical and capacity building support; protected marketing assistance; free working and production space in urban centers in an otherwise tight market for such facilities, etc. Simply put, it is a heavily protected economic sector that has not been subject to rigorous market competition. While such assistance is desirable and even feasible in the short-run, it is extremely difficult to guarantee its continued availability in the long run. This puts the viability and sustainability of the current MSE strategy in question.

7.2.3. Entrepreneurship spirit

The micro-entrepreneur view of the MSE literature indicates that one of the reasons for operators to join the MSE sector is for its flexibility and earning opportunity. Thus operators are believed to be entrepreneurs with the spirit and determination to develop their businesses. Our data showed that operators joined the sector for lack of options and due to high unemployment. These data do not support the entrepreneurial view. Despite this, however, it is quite possible for operators to turn themselves into entrepreneurs once they are in the business. This, however, could be achieved if MSE members and owners tend to be creative and innovative in firm decision-making, including exploring alternative sources of credit, entering the competition arena for markets and firm inputs, applying private sector criteria of profitability to evaluate success, etc. Key informants in different cities have mentioned that there is a tendency on the part of operators to look up to the government to solve many of the problems they face. In short a 'dependency syndrome' among operators and owners is created as a result of the implementation modality.

7.2.4. Inadequate capacity of the MSE sector offices/agencies

While there have been variations among the cities covered in this study, inadequate capacity of MSE sector offices/agencies in the cities visited has repeatedly come up as a constraint in extending assistance to businesses. Many of these bureaus and agencies were found to be lacking in adequately trained organizers and development agents; and the turnover was found to be high. In addition, working conditions and benefits, such as pay rates, were found to be inadequate thus exacerbating the brain drain. The existing staff members are also thinly spread. For example, in one city, there were said to be only 28 development agents and organizers for more than 1400 micro- and small enterprises. Some city governments had initiated reforms to ameliorate the situation but the fruits of these efforts have yet to be seen. For example, in Mekelle city, extension workers are given a different career structure and a salary level one step higher in order to tackle this problem. Despite these attempts, however, the capacity constraint remains a major policy concern which the Federal and Regional governments have to address in unison. Among other things, the need for an institution to provide relevant and practical training to development agents and other personnel working in implementing the MSE development strategy can be considered.

7.3. Policy Issues

7.3.1. The need for private sector involvement in providing micro-finance for MSEs

Within in the Ethiopian context, the issue of micro-finance is a complex one. Among other things, the micro-finance industry is young and undeveloped; and there are several factors constraining its growth. In 2009, there were 29 MFIs in Ethiopia, of which 12 were licensed to operate in Regional states and the rest were licensed to operate nationwide. Most of these provide limited financial service, mainly credit and saving. Their main objective is poverty alleviation and target the lower strata of micro-entrepreneurs. Most of these institutions are inexperienced and follow the same set of micro-lending policies and practices. Most also experience a similar set of problems, including small-loan size, lack of product diversification, lack of flexibility in approach, etc. (Haftu et al. 2009).

Several studies document that availability and supply of adequate micro-finance is critical for the growth and development of small and medium enterprises in Ethiopia. For example, according to the 1995/96 survey of urban informal activities in Ethiopia, lack of working capital was among the most pressing problems that small manufacturing industries identified (the others being marketing and shortage of supply of raw materials) as limiting expansion of their business. The same survey indicated that 50% of the informal sector operators indicated that their main problem in operation was lack of sufficient initial capital. Lack of sufficient capital, particularly at the start of their operations, was also identified as the major problem for about 35% of the small scale manufacturing industries (Gebrehiwot and Wolday 2004)

This study has revealed that micro-finance institutions owned and operated by Regional governments are the sole providers of micro-finance credit to MSEs. The only exception where there is some private sector and NGO involvement in micro-credit finance is in Adama. This, however, is very limited both in scope and coverage. The dominance of the Regional government owned micro-finance institutions in credit provision must give way to a more competitive micro-credit provision and arrangement, at least in the short to medium-term. Simply put, it is necessary to open up opportunities for private sector micro-finance institutions to enter the market of micro-credit provision. This has the twin advantages of increasing choices to beneficiaries and making more capital available to the MSEs. In the long run, however, it is necessary to conduct a comprehensive assessment of the potentials and limitations of the micro-finance sector in the country with the aim of providing feasible policy inputs for the growth of a vibrant micro-finance industry that can assist the government's policy of poverty reduction, employment creation and business development.

7.3.2. Addressing the needs of MSEs

MSEs have specified those constraints which puts them in a disadvantaged situation. Some critical obstacles identified include lack of market, shortage and/or unavailability of finance, shortage of working premise and infrastructure problems. It is important to think of all kinds of innovative mechanisms to alleviate these constraints. For example, in terms of finance, innovative mechanisms other than private sector involvement include encouraging and exploring supplier credit, venture capital, mobilization of own and group finance, etc.

7.3.3. Intensification of promotional activities

In many developing countries such as Ethiopia, information flow is limited and consumers and suppliers rarely meet. There is a dearth of knowledge about prices, products and supplies both on the buyers' and sellers' sides. As a result, MSE operators will not be aware of what is needed and demanded, and consumers will not be aware of what kind of products are available at what prices. Some cities have organized trade fairs for MSEs. This has to be continued and intensified. The businesses themselves, however, should jump into creating this opportunity for themselves jointly. This would remove the pressure from the government and will also encourage private creativity and commitment to marketing and promotion.

7.3.4. Fostering sector-specific support

The present package of support services provided to the MSEs is a standard prescription given to all types of businesses. It is quite possible that different enterprises may require support out of the envisaged packages depending on the nature of the business, its growth stage, etc. A firm, for example, may require support in getting access to electricity, water, etc. These kinds of assistance, for example, are not included in the standard package. Every enterprise has its own unique features. We cannot assume a universal policy that applies uniformly to all categories of MSEs in a similar manner.

7.3.5. Fostering linkages among and between MSEs

The study showed that both vertical and horizontal linkages are poorly developed among MSEs. Cooperation and linkages, however, are key for upgrading. They are also critical in situations where there is capital shortage since through cooperation such as collective purchase and collective marketing, capital shortages could be lessened. In light of its importance, the MSE development strategy has to provide special attention to reduce the isolation of the enterprises and create room for upgrading. Mechanisms to foster linkage with lead firms in a particular sector need to be established. There is also a need to encourage social capital among MSEs so that they forge inter-firm linkage on their own.

7.3.6. Reducing MSE dependency on the government

The MSE strategy is a supply-driven strategy that uses lavish delivery of support services in order to promote growth and reduce poverty. The strategy has created huge demand for support to the businesses. As a result, a huge number of MSE operators are organized but have not started operation. Others who are in the business receive extensive support which is the raison d'etre for their existence. It will be very difficult to sustain this strategy though it might be used as a short-term measure to initiate and promote the sector. This is one possible explanation why there have been very few MSEs that graduated from the sector. It is important to reorient the strategy from massive support to selective and phased strategy and support and transfer the responsibility to the businesses themselves. The enterprises should be responsible for preparing their own business plan, seek training, market, finance and other needs of specific nature.

7.3.7. Given attention to existing MSEs

In principle, the MSE strategy embraces existing and new enterprises in different cities and towns. In practice, however, there is a strong bias towards newly organized businesses by the MSE agencies. The argument for such a bias is that new businesses create new employment and attain the objective of reducing unemployment. These enterprises are in fact more privileged than the existing ones in terms of support services. It is, however, quite important to realize that existing enterprises have equal or more potential in generating employment and they deserve adequate attention. Existing enterprises are already in the business and have been competing and surviving in the market on their own. As they have a track record in the business, it is prudent to support and help existing MSEs grow.

7.3.8. Coordination between the MSE sector and other sectors

The question of how the MSE sector is coordinated and integrated with other sectors of the economy was noted as a major policy issue by key informants. In many instances, it was observed that there were duplication and overlapping of plans and activities by different bureaus and sector offices. For example, there was the need for a clear policy direction as to how rural and agricultural activity in the surrounding areas was to be integrated with the activities of city-based MSEs. There is also a problem of mandate of activities that transcend different sectors. Urban agriculture is a case in point. Though urban agriculture is specified as one of the growth sectors by the MSE strategy, the office of MSE development is not fully capable of supporting the activity in terms of research, technology, etc. Moreover, the promotion of rural-urban linkages, which is one of the objectives of the MSE strategy, requires the integration of agriculture with urban based MSEs in terms of marketing the semi-industrial products and procuring agricultural inputs from the surrounding areas.

Conclusion

The theoretical benefits of MSEs are tremendous. In particular, their suitability for capital-scarce and labor-abundant countries, such as Ethiopia, has been repeatedly stressed in the international literature. The Ethiopian government's objective to promote the sector to serve as a basis for industrialization, reducing poverty and creating employment is in the right direction.

This study has shown that the MSE strategy, as part of the urban development policy, thus far has some positive impacts in improving the livelihoods of beneficiaries and creating employment particularly for the youth and women. This is a very significant achievement and needs to be upheld. The strategy, however, is based on huge support, protection and assistance. The huge support and assistance has a number of implications. First, it has created unrealistic expectations among operators that the demand for assistance is getting out of hand. This has resulted in a number of MSEs not being able to enter the operation stage. Second, it has created a dependency syndrome among operators since they receive lofty support from the government. This discourages the businesses from fending for themselves and aspiring to grow as competitive enterprises that could be a basis for industrialization.

Within the current strategy of MSE development, reforms are needed. For example, selected and phased assistance might do the trick of fostering independence among the enterprises. The universal application of assistance also needs to be changed and sector-specific assistance needs to be promoted. This is fruitful both in terms of using scarce resources and bringing a meaningful change in business operation. A culture of entrepreneurship has to be fostered and promoted if MSEs are to sustain and graduate from small business status. One disadvantage of MSEs is their small size and incapability to compete with more established firms both domestically and internationally. One way of alleviating this constraint is by promoting inter-firm linkages and cooperation. Collective efficiency will be fostered if firms cooperate. Such collective efficiency enhances the competitiveness of enterprises. Moreover, inter-firm linkage helps to make the most out of the value chain from which profits are to be expropriated.

One area that calls for policy attention is the institutional and human resource capacity constraint of MSE bureaus/sector offices. Many of these currently suffer from shortage of well trained staff in several areas. Professional staff that can provide management and technical training and assistance in running the businesses, keeping proper accounting and financial records, preparing appropriate business plans, facilitating marketing arrangements, etc., were found to be in short supply. In addition, high turnover of staff largely caused by not-so-attractive salaries, benefits and poor working conditions, was also said to be a contributory factor. Hence, it becomes a necessity to re-examine the existing policy element with reference to human resource acquisition and management within the sector. Such an initiative must be undertaken within the framework of the broad MSE development strategy to attract and retain an appropriate labor force that will spur the development of the industry.

Future Research Agenda

This study has attempted to assess the contribution of the MSE Strategy of the Ethiopian Government to employment creation, poverty alleviation and business development. In the process, it has been found out that some issues require further investigation and research. The following are some areas of future research:

- The study has found that business expansion may be undermined since there is limited investment by operators in their businesses. More specifically, 63% or nearly two-third use income from the business for household maintenance while only 19% use income for business expansion. Though absence of surplus could be a possible reason for such lack of investment, it is important to further investigate the reasons for disinvestment and possible ways of encouraging investment in the sector by households and individuals.

- Engagement in the MSE sector is expected to increase income and savings and bring about an improvement in welfare. Though the results indicate that some improvements are recorded, there is still some Regional variation in this regard. For example, average savings have declined in Bahir Dar and Hawassa while changes in income are more pronounced in Mekelle and Adama. Although this research has attempted to provide some explanation for this Regional variation, it is necessary to undertake further research that looks at Regional discrepancies to explain the different responses of operators in different Regions.

- The study has focused on MSE beneficiaries to observe changes and sustainability of business development. There is equally a need to study non-beneficiary MSE operators to present a comparative perspective and understand better the changes and sustainability of businesses.

Epilogue

As this publication went to press, it was learnt that the Government of Ethiopia was in the process of revising the draft five-year urban development and industry package to significantly increase youth employment in the country. We hope some of the policy ideas and recommendations that this study provides will be useful inputs in designing a proactive MSE strategy that can promote small business entrepreneurship and reduce poverty and unemployment.

References

Andualem Tegegne. 2004. Challenges in the effective development and promotion of MSEs in Ethiopia: Some suggested approaches. In *Proceedings of the International Workshop on the Role of Micro- and Small Enterprises in the Economic Development of Ethiopia*, edited by Daniel Assefa and Worku Gebeyehu. Addis Ababa.

Asian Development Bank. 1997. *Micro-enterprise development: Not by credit alone.* Manila: Asian Development Bank.

Association of Ethiopian Micro-Finance Institutions. 2002. *Micro- and Small Enterprise (MSE) development in Ethiopia.* Occasional Paper No. 5, March.

Beck, T., Demirgue-Kunt, and R. Levine. 2003. SMEs, growth and poverty. NBER Working Paper 11224.

Carter, Sara, and Dylan Jones-Evans. 2004. "Enterprize and small business principles, practice and policy." Financial Times Press.

Central Statistical Authority (CSA). 1999. Report on large and medium-scale manufacturing and electricity industries survey. *Statistical Bulletin* 210. Addis Ababa, Central Statistical Authority.

_____. 2000. Report on large and medium-scale manufacturing and electricity industries survey. *Statistical Bulletin* 210. Addis Ababa, Central Statistical Authority.

Chibwe, Chisala. 2008. Unlocking the potential of Zambian micro, small and medium enterprises: Learning from the international best practice. Discussion Paper No.134. Japan: Institute of Developing Economies.

Dipta, Wayan I. 2004. Indonesia experiences on supporting new and existing SMEs. Ministry for Cooperatives and SMEs, Jakarta.

Eshetu Bekele and Zeleke Worku. 2008. Women entrepreneurship in micro, small and medium enterprises: The case of Ethiopia. *Journal of International Women's Studies* 10, 2 (November): 3.

Eversole, Robyn. 2004. Solving poverty for yourself: Micro-enterprise development, micro-finance and migration. Hyderbad, India: Icfar University Press.

Fasika Damte and Daniel Ayalew. 1997. Financing Micro- and Small-Scale Enterprises: An empirical survey in urban Ethiopia. *Ethiopian Journal of Economics* VI, no.1 (April).

Federal Democratic Republic of Ethiopia (FDRE). 1997. Micro- and Small Enterprise Development Strategy. Ministry of Trade and Industry (MoTI).

Gebrehiwot Ageba and Wolday Amha. 2004. Micro- and Small Enterprises development in Ethiopia: Survey report. Addis Ababa: Ethiopian Development Research Institute.

Haftu Berihun, Tsehaye Tsegaye, Teklu Kidane and Tassew W/Hanna. 2009. *Financial needs of micro-and small enterprise operators in Ethiopia.* Occasional Paper No. 24. Addis Ababa: Association of Ethiopian Micro-finance Institutions.

Harvie, C. 2003. The contribution of micro-enterprise to economic recovery and poverty alleviation in East Asia. University of Wollogong, Faculty of Economics Working Paper. http://ro.uow.edu.au/commwkpapers/73

Hawkins, H. 1998. Economic and financial developments in 1998. *Humphrey-Hawkins Report,* July 21.

Institut national de la Statistique et de la Demographie (INSD). 1993. Burkina Faso.

Kula, Olaf, Vikas Choudhary, and Lisa Batzdorff. 2005. Micro report: Integrating micro- and small enterprises into productive markets. *Micro-Links.*

Menash, J.V, Michael Tribe, and John Weiss. 2007. The small scale manufacturing sector in Ghana: A source of dynamism or of subsistence income? *Journal of International Development* 19: 253-273.

Ministry of Finance and Economic Development (MoFED). 2006. Plan for Sustained and Accelerated Development to End Poverty (OASDEP). Federal Democratic Republic of Ethiopia.

Ministry of Works and Urban Development (MoWUD). 2007. The Urban Development and Industry Package. Federal Democratic Republic of Ethiopia.

Moser, C., and Jeremy Holland. 2008. Household responses to poverty and vulnerability. Vol. 4. Wahsington, D.C.: World Bank.

Nelson, Candace. 2000. Microenterprise development in the United States: An overview. Microenterprise Factsheet Series, no. 1. Aspen Institute, Microenterprise Fund for Innovation, Effectiveness, Learning, and Dissemination, Arlington, Va.

Orlando, M.B., and M. Pollack. 2000. Microenterprises and poverty: Evidence from Latim America. Inter-American Development Bank, Washington, D.C.

Salmon, J.U. 2004. Micro-business and employment generation for poverty reduction. Workshop on Science and Technology, March 3-5.

Schreiner, M., and Gary Woller. 2003. Micro-enterprise development program in the US and in the developing countries. *World Development* 31(9).

Shrestha, Nabina. (n.d.). Empowerment of the poor through micro-enterprise development in Nepal.

Tegegne Gebre-Egziabher. 2007. Geographically differentiated strategy, urbanization agenda and rural-urban linkages: Emerging Regional development strategies in Ethiopia. *Regional Development Dialogue* 28 (1).

Tegegne Gebre-Egziabher and Mulat Demeke. 2005. Micro-enterprises performance in small towns of Amhara Region: Implications for local economic development. In *Local economic development in Africa: Enterprises, communities and local government*, edited by Tegegne Gebre-Egziabher and Helmsing Bert. Netherlands: Shaker Publishing.

Thapa, Ajay. 2007. Micro-enterprises and household income. *The Journal of Nepalese Business Studies* IV (1).

UNCTAD. 2005. Growing micro and small enterprises in LDCs - The "missing middle" in LDCs: Why micro and small enterprises are not growing.

USAID. 2008. SME lending in Africa: Challenges, current trends and USAID initiatives. Washington, D.C.

Wolday Amha. 2002. *The role of finance and Business Development Service (BDS) in Micro- and Small Enterprise (MSE) development in Ethiopia.* Occasional Paper No. 5. Addis Ababa: Association of Ethiopian Microfinance Institutions.

Annex
List of Persons Interviewed

Adama

1. Ato Diriba Tadesse, Process Owner, Adama City MSE Office
2. Ato Tadele Shigute, Head, Mayor's Secretariat Office
3. Ato Adugna Legesse, Kebele 09, Generalist
4. Ato Teshome Wolde, Organizer, City MSE Office
5. Ato Jemal Abdel, Kebele 05, Team Leader
6. W/o Alemaya Berhane, Kebele 08, Generalist

Hawassa

1. Ato Belay Bekele, Coordinator, Hawassa MSE Bureau
2. Ato Hailu Birru, Generalist, Regional Trade and Industry Bureau
3. Ato Samuel Otoro, Organizer, Tabor Sub-city
4. Ato Alemayehu Denbi, Trade and Industry Bureau
5. Ato Berta Dawit, Addis Ketema Sub-city Development Agent
6. Ato Tamrat Tariku, Omo Microfinance;
7. Ato Tafesse Firra, Menaheria Sub-city;
8. Ato Behailu Mohammed, Mehal Ketema Sub-city, Organizer
9. Ato Bereket Mehari, Yem Sub-city, Development Agent.

Bahir Dar

1. Ato Tefera Tadios, Head, Regional MSE Secretariat.
2. Ato Asfaw Abebe, Process Owner, Bahir Dar City MSE Office

Mekelle
1. Ato Yemane Mahfud, Head, Bureau of Finance and Economic Development
2. Ato Yemane W/Gebriel, Regional MSE Process Owner

www.ingramcontent.com/pod-product-compliance
Lightning Source LLC
Chambersburg PA
CBHW080002280326

41935CB00013B/1720